Contents

THE holocaust in Gaza has been reignited after a brief intermission. The bodies are piling up again. Food is running out. Netanyahu and Trump are working to end the existence of Palestinians in their historic homeland.

The suffering is unfathomable. And it's all being supported by the western empire under which we live.

It's up to each of us how we're going to respond to this nightmare. This month's issue of JOHNSTONE features UN Special Rapporteur Francesca Albanese, because she is an exemplary embodiment of what it looks like to live a life that answers this urgent call.

All works are written by Caitlin Johnstone and Tim Foley. The Caitlin Johnstone project is 100 percent reader-funded. Cover is an original oil portrait of Francesca Albanese by Caitlin Johnstone.

Visit caitlinjohnst.one for the original articles and their supporting links.

You Cannot Separate Yourself From What's Happening In Gaza

The Gaza holocaust has reignited with as much sadistic fury as it ever saw under the Biden administration. More than five hundred people have reportedly been killed by Israeli bombardment since the onslaught resumed early Tuesday morning, including at least 200 children and 112 women.

I will admit to having been hopeful. I know it's illegal to express hope online, but I really did hope that by some miracle peace would find some way forward in Gaza in spite of the frenetic efforts by Trump and Netanyahu and their cohorts to sabotage it. I had hope, and now I have grief.

Now this constant mass atrocity has been fully reanimated. And the people who rule over us are actively supporting this, while working to imprison, fire, silence and deport anyone who opposes it.

This is a broken civilization. A warped and twisted dystopia. The waking nightmare we are witnessing in Gaza is the result of everything that we have become as a society. Those dead and mutilated children on your social media feed are the fruit on the tree of the western world.

Please understand that this is personal now. This isn't only about some strangers in the middle east. It's also about you. It's about your rights. It's about your freedom to speak out against the criminality of your rulers. It's about the kind of society you want to live in. It's about the kind of future you want for your children.

We are not separate from what's happening in Gaza, as hard as we might try to make ourselves feel that way. Gaza is here. The waves of blood are lapping at your doorstep. The dead and mutilated children are strewn about your living room and kitchen. They were placed there by the powerful people who run your government and its allies.

There's no getting away from it. Gaza has been brought right to you and laid at your feet.

And it's up to you how you're going to respond to it.

Featured image via Wikemedia Commons/UNRWA.

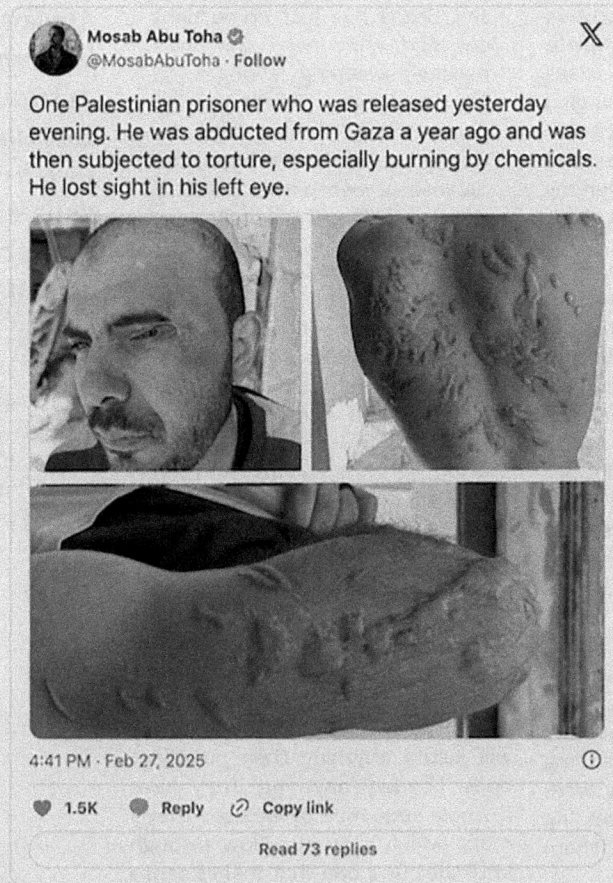

Palestinian Hostage Released With Obvious Torture Scars; Western Press Ignores Him
•Notes From The Edge Of The Narrative Matrix•

A Palestinian man who was held captive by Israel for over a year has been released with horrific scarring all over his body. The man, Mohammed Abu Tawila, told local media that the marks came from his captors pouring acid and other chemicals onto his skin in order to torture him. One of his eyes was also destroyed, reportedly in a savage beating.

You think you've seen the worst thing you can possibly see in this ever-unfolding nightmare, and then you see something like this.

And of course the western press has nothing to say about it. If an Israeli hostage were returned with these signs of torture the entire western political-media class would demand that everyone in Gaza be exterminated with poison gas. But he's Palestinian, so they ignore him.

•

It's weird how Israel's supporters will just pretend to believe complete nonsense in order to advance Israeli agendas. Oh yeah, Hamas strangled those redheads with their bare hands! OMG Hamas beheaded babies and roasted them in ovens! Oh no, Jeremy Corbyn is a Nazi! We totally believe these things!

And what's even weirder is they expect you to pretend to believe they're not pretending. If you come out and say something like "Okay but surely nobody actually believes Hamas has been hiding in every hospital in Gaza," they'll flip out at you. If you point out that it's much more likely the Bibas family was killed by Israeli airstrikes in an area where women and children were getting killed by Israeli airstrikes every day than that the Israeli government is telling the truth about something they lie about constantly just as a critical ceasefire deadline approaches, you'll be swarmed by Israel supporters not only pretending to be absolutely certain they were murdered by Hamas, but demanding that you pretend to take them seriously.

It's just so silly. These freaks act out these ridiculous stage plays where they pretend to be outraged about bogus atrocity propaganda or pretend to "feel unsafe" because of some completely made-up antisemitism crisis, and everyone knows they're fulla shit, but we're supposed to pretend we don't know that or we're the worst person in the universe.

This is a bunch of grown adults rolling around on the floor having manipulative tantrums about made-up nonsense and then having tantrums at anyone who doesn't take their tantrums seriously. It's like, come on. Have a little dignity. Where is your self-respect? Is advancing Israeli information interests and facilitating foreign land grabs really worth debasing yourself like this?

Just about the cringiest, most embarrassing thing I've ever witnessed.

•

Jeff Bezos has just come right out and announced that he's making sweeping changes to The Washington Post's opinion pages, saying, "We are going to be writing every day in support and defense of two pillars: personal liberties and free markets."

In other words, he's going to have his news outlet's opinion pages dominated by people arguing in support of unfettered capitalism. One of the richest people in the world bought one of the most influential newspapers in the world to turn it into an even bigger capitalist propaganda rag than it already was.

•

After four years and one month observing how Trump supporters behave while their cult leader is in power I can confidently say that they will justify anything their president does. Literally anything. They have a whole sequence of excuses they'll make which they just flow through until they find one that makes sense to them. In justifying any ugly thing their president does, the excuses go as follows:

1. What Trump did is good.

2. If what Trump did is not good, then it was actually a brilliant strategic 4D chess maneuver designed to advance the greater good in the long term.

3. If no discernible good can come of it in the long term, then he was just trolling.

4. If he wasn't just trolling, then the Deep State made him do it. You can't just go against the Deep State, you know. What kind of naive idiot are you?

•

Amnesty International has formally denounced Australian universities for adopting an insane and speech-stifling definition of antisemitism to assist Israeli ethnic cleansing agendas. So at least that's something.

•

Oh, and a humble observation: if people protesting genocide and ethnic cleansing makes you "feel unsafe", then perhaps you are the fucking problem.

•

Trump Sends Netanyahu Weapons While Talking Tough To Zelensky

Israeli media are now reporting that Benjamin Netanyahu is considering "a brief resumption" of the onslaught in Gaza in order to pressure Hamas to make concessions and change the terms of the ceasefire agreement which was signed on the 19th of January.

The Times of Israel reports:

"Prime Minister Benjamin Netanyahu is considering a brief resumption of fighting against Hamas to pressure the terror group into making further concessions, according to an Israeli television report aired Saturday as he held high-level deliberations on the stalled negotiations to advance to the second stage of the hostage-ceasefire agreement in Gaza.

"Hamas has rejected Israel's proposal to extend the first, 42-day stage of the deal, which formally expires Saturday night, insisting that the deal proceed with phase two, which Israel has largely refused to negotiate for the past month. Thirty-three Israeli hostages were released, eight of them dead, in exchange for nearly 2,000 Palestinian prisoners. Five Thai nationals held hostage in the Gaza Strip were freed separately.

"With the ceasefire expected to lapse at midnight, Netanyahu and Defense Minister Israel Katz will meet Sunday, along with other security officials, to discuss preparations for a potential resumption of fighting in Gaza and a review of all potential war fronts, Channel 12 news reported."

This framing that Hamas has "rejected" Israel's proposed extension of phase one is just the current propaganda line from the US-Israeli PR machine. In reality the terms of the ceasefire deal say that Israel and Hamas were supposed to move on to phase two of the agreement this weekend, but Israel has been refusing to negotiate the second stage of the agreement this entire time because it would entail a withdrawal of Israeli troops and a commitment to a lasting peace. This idea that the first phase of the ceasefire should be "extended" instead of continuing on to the second phase is a brand new proposition the US and Israel just started pushing a few days ago.

It is therefore Israel who is rejecting the ceasefire as written and trying to write up new terms for the deal; Hamas is just insisting on the terms of the ceasefire it agreed to.

But today we're being hammered with this message that Hamas is rejecting peace. A tweet by Axios' Israeli intelligence operative Barak Ravid reads as follows:

"Israeli Prime Minister's office says Israel agreed to a U.S. proposal for extending the Gaza ceasefire in return for release of hostages but claims Hamas refuses."

So that's the official message we're being fed by the consent-manufacturing machine, as the Trump administration sends even more weapons to Israel. The White House has just used its "emergency powers" to bypass congressional oversight for a $3 billion weapons transfer to the Netanyahu regime, right after posturing as a stern tough guy who cares about making peace in his controversial dustup with Ukrainian president Volodymyr Zelensky.

As readers have no doubt already heard, the entire western political-media class has been in an uproar since Trump and Vice President JD Vance made international headlines by publicly raking Zelensky over the coals for his role in obstructing peace with Russia, even accusing him of "gambling with World War Three."

Democrats are rending their garments over the public humiliation of Saint Zelensky and crying about the "bullying" behavior of Trump and Vance, while Republicans are applauding the whole ordeal as a sign that Trump is a strong and heroic peacemaker who doesn't take any guff from Washington's warmongering proxies. But the most immediate and glaring point about Zelensky's public castigation is that this same administration doesn't appear to be taking that same energy to Benjamin Netanyahu as he prepares to resume a genocide.

And of course it doesn't. Trump has publicly admitted to being bought and owned by the world's wealthiest Israeli, megadonor Miriam Adelson, while JD Vance is the protégé of virulent Zionist billionaire Peter Thiel. What we witnessed on Friday was Trump speaking to Zelensky in public the way Adelson probably speaks to Trump in private. We can certainly never expect to see him speaking that way to Netanyahu.

It is good that things are moving toward peace in Ukraine, but this war was never intended to be permanent. It was only ever intended to be a temporary quagmire to bleed and divert Russia as much as possible while advancing strategic objectives elsewhere, which we recently saw manifest in the empire's successful regime change operation in Syria. Zelensky, like every other US imperial asset, was only ever intended to be used and then discarded. The gears of the imperial war machine roll onward.

Featured image via Wikimedia Commons/The White House (Public Domain).

Israel Begins Choking Gaza Again, Backed By Adelson Stooge Trump

Israel has once again laid siege to Gaza, this time in full coordination with the Trump administration. All goods are being blocked from entering the enclave, including humanitarian aid. This comes after a 15-month US-backed Israeli bombing campaign deliberately made it impossible for people to survive in Gaza without extensive amounts of aid.

The move is an effort to pressure Hamas into changing the terms of the ceasefire deal they agreed to in January by shifting to a new Trump administration plan to extend the first phase of the deal instead of negotiating the second stage as scheduled.

So Israel is breaking international laws against collective punishment by laying siege to an aid-dependent population in order to force changes to a ceasefire deal. You might assume such a straightforward act of psychopathic criminality would be correctly conveyed by the headlines of the western press, but if you assumed such a thing you are adorably naive.

As we anticipated yesterday, the official western propaganda line is spinning this to blame Hamas for rejecting a peace deal, but some of the headlines have been even worse than I would have guessed.

"Hamas rejects extending first phase of Gaza ceasefire, ties hostage release to phased deal," reads a headline from Reuters.

"Israel halts aid to Gaza as Hamas rejects revised ceasefire proposal," says the Financial Times.

"Israel says it will block aid going into Gaza until Hamas agrees to ceasefire extension," says CNN.

"Israel Halts All Aid Into Gaza as Cease-Fire Expires," says The New York Times in its signature passive-voice framing.

"Israeli PM Benjamin Netanyahu presses for Gaza ceasefire extension," reads a particularly obnoxious headline about the story from Australia's state broadcaster ABC.

To be clear, it is Israel who is rejecting the ceasefire, not Hamas. Hamas already agreed to a ceasefire, and has been honoring it. It is Israel who is pushing to change the terms of the deal instead of moving forward with the deal as agreed. Israel is doing this because moving ceasefire negotiations on to their second stage would entail moving toward a commitment to lasting peace and the removal of Israeli troops from Gaza.

A new deal isn't even necessary to extend the first phase of the ceasefire; as Muhammad Shehada noted on Twitter, phase one would renew automatically as long as phase two negotiations are ongoing. Phase one of the ceasefire isn't the issue here: killing phase two is.

And it's important to understand that Netanyahu never intended to move forward to the second phase of the ceasefire. As soon as the agreement was signed in January the Netanyahu-aligned factions of the Israeli press were already asserting that the prime minister would never allow the ceasefire to move on to phase two. In early February the Israeli outlet Haaretz reported that according to insider sources Netanyahu intended to sabotage the ceasefire before it could move to its second stage.

It's important to be aware that Netanyahu always intended to sabotage the ceasefire because it shows that none of the reasons being given for Israel's actions today are the real reasons. It has nothing to do with hostages. It has nothing to do with anything Hamas has done since the signing of the agreement. It has nothing to do with the Bibas family. Those aren't the reasons, they're the excuses. The excuses for Netanyahu to do what he always intended to do.

It's probably also worth noting at this juncture that Donald Trump has publicly admitted to being bought and owned by the world's wealthiest Israeli, virulent Zionist Miriam Adelson. The president openly acknowledged on the campaign trail that the first time he was president, Miriam Adelson and her late husband Sheldon were at the White House "probably almost more than anybody" demanding favors for Israel like moving the US embassy to Jerusalem and acknowledging Israel's illegitimate claim to the Golan Heights, which he eagerly granted. Miriam Adelson gave the Trump campaign $100 million last year.

It used to be considered an antisemitic conspiracy theory to say that Trump is controlled by Adelson cash; back in 2020 Roger Waters was internationally denounced as an evil Jew hater for saying what Trump himself openly admitted to last year. Now here we are, watching Trump rush weapons to Israel and push to permanently ethnically cleanse Gaza of all Palestinians while Netanyahu happily commits war crimes in full confidence that he will be supported by the Adelson asset in the White House.

Featured image via Dan Scavino/The White House (Public Domain).

Some Thoughts On Ukraine

As the Trump administration pauses military aid to Ukraine and western liberals continue their shrieking meltdown over Trump hurting Saint Zelensky's feelings, it's probably worth reminding everyone that the Russian invasion of Ukraine was indisputably provoked by western aggressions. That's why so many western experts and analysts spent years warning ahead of time that western aggressions were going to provoke an invasion of Ukraine.

Now, some may hear this and say "Okay but Russia still shouldn't have invaded even though our western leaders were aggressively provoking them to." But before you do that it might be a good idea to look inside yourself and ask where that impulse is arising from. Why are you so eager to skip past the part where you criticize your own rulers for their role in starting this war and focus solely on criticizing the leader of an eastern government who has no power over you? What is it inside of you that's flailing all over the place trying to avoid any forceful scrutiny of the reckless warmongering of your own government and its allies?

The last time a foreign rival placed a credible military threat near the border of the United States, the US responded so aggressively that the world almost ended (if you want to know just how close we came to nuclear annihilation during the Cuban Missile Crisis, look up the name Vasili Arkhipov). Western liberals have been conditioned to insist that Russia should have responded differently to the US empire amassing proxy forces on its border than the US would respond to the same kind of threat on its own borders. The frenetic mental contortions needed to justify this ridiculous double standard are only possible because the west is saturated in domestic propaganda manipulating the way they think about the world.

It makes sense for there to be criticism of Russia for its role in this war, and for people to be horrified by the nightmare that's been happening in Ukraine these last few years. What makes absolutely no sense whatsoever is for western liberals (or "progressives" or whatever they want to call themselves) to assign ZERO PERCENT RESPONSIBILITY to their own government and its allies for their extensively documented role in sparking this conflict and ONE HUNDRED PERCENT RESPONSIBILITY to a foreign government with no power over them. That's pathetic, bootlicking behavior, and it's utterly inexcusable.

Stop performing mental gymnastics to defend the abuses of your rulers. Have a little dignity for god's sake.

It is good that Trump appears to be moving toward ending an unwinnable proxy war that Ukrainians no longer want to fight. Anyone who disagrees with this is a dogshit human being.

I am not grateful to Trump for ending this nightmare, I'm just disgusted with anyone who's against doing so. The proxy war in Ukraine was going to end sometime relatively soon anyway; the only way for NATO to reverse Russia's steady gains at this point would be to intervene more directly in ways that would risk nuclear consequences that western leaders aren't willing to receive. This was always a chess game for them; they're not going to put their own necks on the line. So the war had to end to make way for other imperial projects — the Trumpists are just the faction that the empire has tasked with advancing this agenda.

I will not waste any gratitude on Trump rolling back a failed imperial bid to weaken Russia, but I will absolutely scream my fucking lungs out at anyone who insists Ukrainians should keep throwing their bodies into a war that Ukrainians themselves no longer support. If you want the Ukraine war to continue, then go enlist and put your body on the line so that Ukrainians don't have to. The Ukrainian Foreign Legion is still accepting volunteers. If you want this horrific war to continue, either go and fight or shut the fuck up. Stop tweeting from the sofa in your safe, comfortable home and get your ass to the frontline. Bring along as many western liberals as you can convince to join your cause.

The western empire provoked this war. The western empire sabotaged peace talks in the early weeks after the invasion. They refused off-ramp after off-ramp in pushing Ukraine into this situation, and as a result Ukraine is going to be much worse off than before this all started. Wanting Ukraine to keep throwing human lives into the meat grinder in the hopes that they can recover all their lost territory is just sunk cost fallacy at this point.

Ukrainians now recognize that it's time to cut their losses and negotiate a peace. Western armchair warriors need to recognize this too.

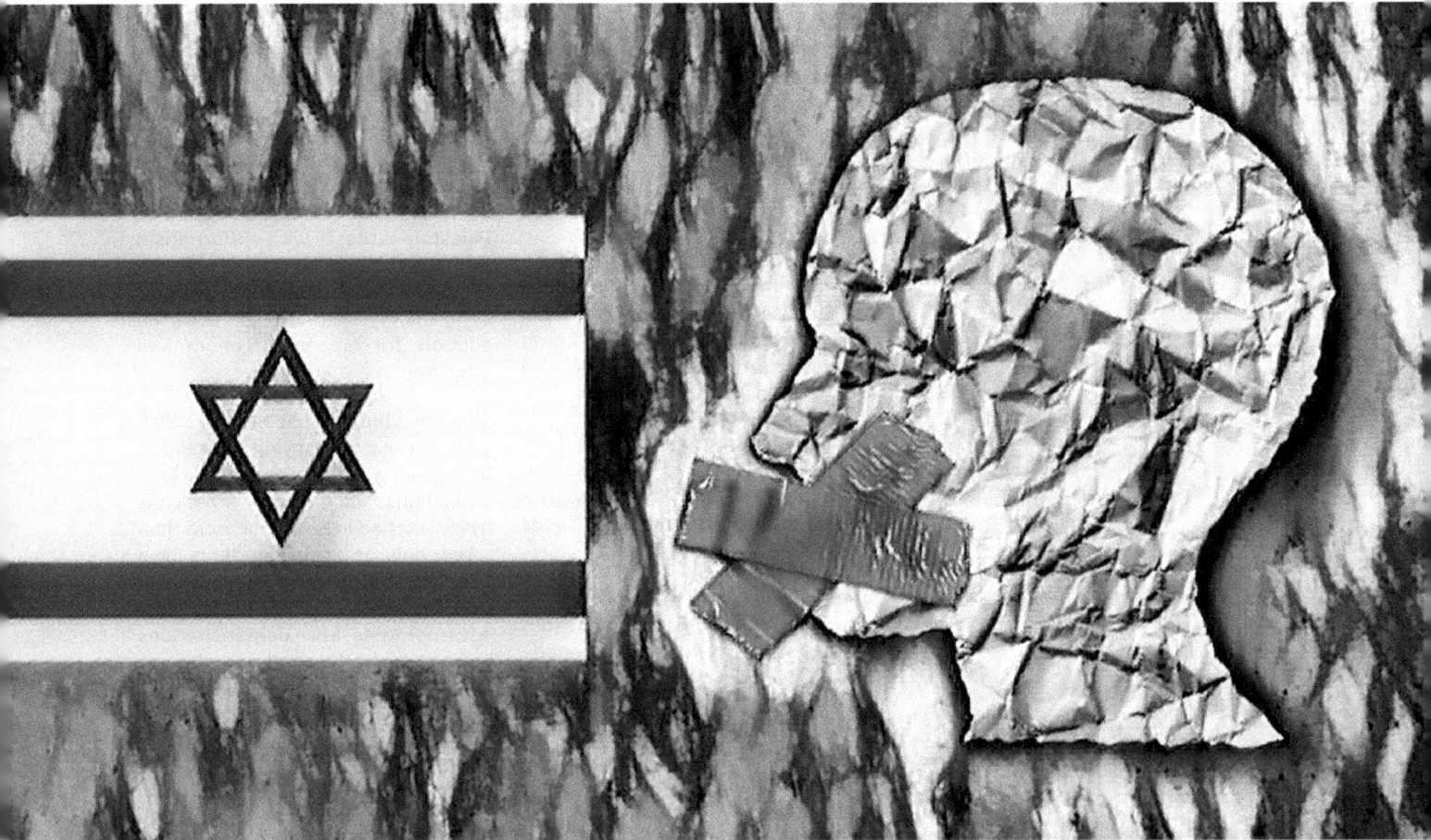

The West's Support For Israel Is The #1 Threat To Free Speech

President Trump has made a post on Truth Social saying federal funding will be cut to universities which allow "illegal protests" on their campuses, obliquely referring to pro-Palestine demonstrations against Israel's genocidal atrocities.

"All Federal Funding will STOP for any College, School, or University that allows illegal protests," Trump said. "Agitators will be imprisoned/or permanently sent back to the country from which they came. American students will be permanently expelled or, depending on on the crime, arrested. NO MASKS!"

Elise Stefanik, Trump's nominee for ambassador to the UN, made it clear that this was the Trump administration taking a position on "anti-Israel hate."

"Antisemitism and anti-Israel hate will not be tolerated on American campuses," tweeted Stefanik with a screenshot of Trump's Truth Social post.

Trump's declaration follows a completely insane statement from health secretary Robert F Kennedy Jr which makes the targeting of pro-Palestine protests much more explicit.

"Anti-Semitism — like racism — is a spiritual and moral malady that sickens societies and kills people with lethalities comparable to history's most deadly plagues," said Kennedy. "In recent years, the censorship and false narratives of woke cancel culture have transformed our great universities into greenhouses for this deadly and virulent pestilence. Making America healthy means building communities of trust and mutual respect, based on speech freedom and open debate."

Leaving aside Kennedy's ridiculous claim that antisemitism "kills people with lethalities comparable to history's most deadly plagues" in modern times and all the weird mental contortions he's performing to turn this into a Health and Human Services issue, conflating pro-Palestine protests with antisemitism and then claiming it needs to be eliminated as a "pestilence" squarely contradicts Kennedy's asserted support for "speech freedom and open debate."

Kennedy's bat shit crazy remarks align with an accompanying statement from Secretary of Education Linda McMahon, who says, "Americans have watched in horror for more than a year now, as Jewish students have been assaulted and harassed on elite university campuses. Unlawful encampments and demonstrations have completely paralyzed day-to-day campus operations, depriving Jewish students of learning opportunities to which they are entitled."

They are using the completely fictional narrative of "antisemitism" on university campuses to stomp out protests against Israeli atrocities in the United States. They couldn't be more transparent about it. Which is why civil rights groups like the American Civil Liberties Union (ACLU) and the Foundation for Individual Rights and Expression (FIRE) immediately released statements denouncing this move by the Trump administration.

"It is disturbing to see the White House threatening freedom of speech and academic freedom on U.S. college campuses so blatantly," said Cecillia Wang, legal director of the ACLU. "We stand in solidarity with university leaders in their commitment to free speech, open debate, and peaceful dissent on campus. Trump's latest coercion campaign, attempting to turn university administrators against their own students and faculty, harkens back to the McCarthy era and is at odds with American constitutional values and the basic mission of universities."

"Today's message will cast an impermissible chill on student protests about the Israeli-Palestinian conflict," says FIRE. "Paired with President Trump's 2019 executive order adopting an unconstitutional definition of anti-Semitism, and his January order threatening to deport international students for engaging in protected expression, students will rationally fear punishment for wholly protected political speech."

If you support freedom of speech you now have an ethical obligation to oppose Israel, even if you didn't before.

Western governments' support for Israel is the biggest threat to free speech in our society today. Civil rights are being stomped out throughout the western world to protect Israeli information interests, and speech is being suppressed in support of Israel more aggressively than with any other topic. We're not seeing this level of all-out warfare against free expression on any other frontline — not Russia, not vaccines, not "election security", not on any kind of ideological front. The west's support for Israel is the number one threat to free speech in the west today, and nothing else comes anywhere close.

Trump's latest announcement about "illegal protests" against Israel on university campuses is just the latest escalation in what has been an ongoing assault on all criticism of the Zionist entity. We're seeing journalists and activists persecuted and fired for opposing Israel's genocidal atrocities in Gaza, protests violently shut down by police, new laws shoved through at alarming speed to help target pro-Palestine demonstrators, massive amounts of social media censorship across all major platforms — all while the mainstream press commit extremely egregious journalistic malpractice with obfuscations in their reporting and punditry designed to spin Israel's abuses in a positive light.

Even if you've never cared about Israel before, you should be opposing it if you care about the existence of free speech in your society. Hell, you should be aggressively resisting this war on speech even if you support Israel. When civil liberties are being snuffed out one by one with increasing brazenness in defense of a foreign state, then everyone who claims to stand for freedom has an obligation to stand against it.

Featured image via Adobe Stock.

Trump's Demented Gaza Threats, And Other Notes From The Edge Of The Narrative Matrix

In a statement addressed "to the People of Gaza," President Trump warned on Wednesday that "A beautiful Future awaits, but not if you hold Hostages. If you do, you are DEAD!"

Again, this was explicitly addressed to the entirety of Gaza's population, not only to Hamas. US presidents kill civilians all the time, but it's highly unusual for them to explicitly threaten a civilian population with extermination in a statement addressed directly to them; you have to go back to the leaflets President Truman dropped on Japan warning of nuclear annihilation in 1945 to find anything like this.

At the same time, Israel is reportedly preparing a "hell plan" in which it will resume its genocidal onslaught and cut Gaza off from electricity and water if Hamas refuses to accept Israel's revised terms for the ceasefire deal in the coming days. The plan to cut off water is especially terrifying, as it would lead to mass civilian deaths relatively quickly.

●

All of Trump supporters' reasons for supporting Trump are invalidated by his positions on Israel.

"He puts America first" — he puts Israel first.

"He's making peace" — he's assisting Israel's mass murder and tyranny.

"He supports free speech" — but not speech which criticizes Israel.

●

The current Israel apologist line on the IDF's siege on Gaza is that Israel isn't obligated to feed people it's at war with, which is idiotic in a couple of different ways.

Firstly, saying Israel doesn't have to feed Gaza is like saying you don't have to feed the people in a prison or a hospital. Yes you obviously do you psychopath, it's an area you've enclosed and made fully dependent on outside aid.

But also, Israel doesn't even feed Gaza. They're currently stopping other people from feeding Gaza, which is like putting security outside of a hospital or prison to make sure nobody can bring in the essential aid you're not providing.

●

Sixty-one Palestinian detainees have reportedly died since October 7 because of the cruel treatment they receive at the hands of their captors. Israeli hostages died because Israel was dropping bombs and laying siege on the place where the prisoners were, while Palestinian hostages are dying because Israel tortures, rapes, starves and abuses them. Israel kills Palestinian hostages and Israeli hostages.

●

People tell me "Caitlin I like what you say about Gaza, but I hate what you say about Ukraine!"

Okay well that's because you're only partially awake to the abuses of the western empire. Gaza is much, much easier to understand than Ukraine. You've still got a lot of learning to do.

●

I can understand why some antiwar people backed Trump over Harris; there were arguments to be made that he was the lesser warmonger. What I cannot understand is how anyone who seeks peace can continue defending him now that he's in office, though. It's just bootlicking at this point.

Defending Trump by babbling about how bad Kamala Harris was is like defending the US invasion of Iraq by saying "Oh so I guess you wish Hitler had won WWII." The election is in the past. It was four months ago. It has no relevance to current criticisms of Trump's actions.

It annoys me how Trumpers will do this in anti-war circles. The other day I criticized the president's actions in Gaza and got multiple MAGA people in my mentions babbling about Kamala Harris. It's like, who? I've practically forgotten who Harris even is. I'm busy criticizing the actual empire as it actually presently exists. If Harris had won I'd be criticizing her, but she didn't, so I focus on Trump. That's what anyone who isn't a blind partisan bootlicker would do.

They did this throughout Trump's first term with Hillary Clinton. "Okay sure his Yemen veto was bad but I'd rather have him than Hillary." Okay, so? Why are you interrupting important criticisms of the powerful to prattle about an irrelevant former Democratic presidential candidate? How could you possibly even think that's something worth saying?

No matter how bad Kamala Harris or Hillary Clinton were, it doesn't magically make Trump good. That's like thinking cancer is good just because heart disease is bad. It's shitbrained thinking, and it's become a real pet peeve of mine.

•

In the west we have the saying "talk is cheap", but what's funny is that there's absolutely nothing in western society that reflects this as our actual position. The politicians who talk the biggest talk are the ones who get into power. The promotions, investments and business loans go to the people who talk the best game. Our whole society is perpetually marinating in propaganda where skillful manipulators use words to influence the way people think, speak, vote, work, spend, and behave at mass scale.

Talk is not cheap in western society. Talk is highly valued and handsomely rewarded. Talk is our most prized product.

Interestingly I have read that in China the exact opposite is the case. Very little value is placed on talk. The politicians who are elevated to prominence are the ones who have proved themselves with accomplishments over the years. Western businessmen sometimes struggle in China because their whole careers they've learned that making big deals comes down to talking big talk, but Chinese businesses are only interested in whether you have a solid track record of coming through with the goods. Even between family members and romantic partnerships there's a lot less emphasis on saying "I love you" and a lot more emphasis on showing your love with deeds, because in China, talk really is cheap.

And funny enough that's how we're seeing things play out on the world stage: the west pouring immense amounts of resources into propaganda, cultural domination and soft power influence operations while China quietly surges ahead in more and more fields every year. We're talking while China is doing.

Featured image via the POTUS X account.

If You Want To Fight The Machine, Don't Move To The Right

People in politics and media who oppose the status quo often drift rightward, especially in the US. Tulsi Gabbard and RFK Jr are some clear recent examples, but you see it happen all the time.

This is because the Trumpian political wing offers mainstream power and influence to those with an "anti-establishment" streak, while mainstream progressive politics doesn't offer anything close. If you're a right wing "populist" you can get elected president, while anyone to the left of Kamala Harris sees their campaigns sabotaged with smears and rigged primaries.

We see a similar dynamic play out in independent media; you'll see many solidly leftist commentators drifting to the right as they find bigger numbers in attacking liberal institutions than attacking the Trumpian faction, because anti-establishment sentiment is much more mainstream on the right. A much larger audience pool has been allowed to amass there for hostility toward establishment institutions — because the right poses no threat to real power.

And therein lies the key point. Anti-establishment figures in politics and punditry aren't drifting rightward because the right has better arguments or is more solidly grounded in truth and morality, they're drifting rightward because the so-called "populist right" has been allowed to flourish while its mirror on the left has not. Right wing "populism" has been allowed to flourish by the very power structures its proponents purport to oppose, while the authentic left has been systematically dismantled by generations of aggressive imperial operations (look up COINTELPRO for example). That's why you see Trump backed by oligarchs, empire managers and DC swamp monsters and see Trumpism uplifted by the Murdoch press, while anti-imperialist socialism can barely even be said to exist anywhere in the US-aligned world.

So while the power and influence offered by right wing "populist" factions can be tempting, that power and influence only exists because those factions are supported and defended by the empire itself. Public discontent is being corralled toward establishment-friendly political structures so that it doesn't head anywhere that can threaten the mechanics of the empire, while authentic opposition to capitalism, militarism and empire building is viciously subverted by any means necessary. Bernie Sanders and AOC play the same role on the other side of the aisle, by the way, as do ostensibly leftist media like TYT who herd people back into support for the Democratic Party.

Real opposition to real power is not permitted to ascend to the presidency of the world's most powerful government. It is marginalized, smeared and subverted, and kept as small as possible. That's why some who begin with sincere opposition to real power find themselves drawn to the right: it's larger and offers more opportunities, because it is more aligned with the ruling power structures of our day.

It's fool's gold. It sells you power and influence so that you can fight the power, but after you've made that bargain you find yourself on the same side as the power. You sold out for nothing. You might as well have skipped the middle part and gone directly to collecting the big bucks whoring yourself out to mainstream politics and media defending the empire without pretending to be something else.

Staying true and authentic can be hard. It comes at a price. You don't get to see your favorite politicians win elections and take important positions in government. You don't get to amass tens of millions of loyal followers who hang on your every word. You lose friends and alienate family members with your positions on war and capitalism and imperialism and Zionism. You can't even watch a movie or a show without being frequently disgusted by the empire propaganda you'll see. It isn't pretty. But at least it's real.

It's another one of those red pill vs blue pill deals. Do you want disconcerting truths or comforting lies? If you want to be true to what's true, you don't compromise your values to support political factions which help prop up the very power structures you oppose. You stay focused on the enemy. You keep throwing sand in the gears of the machine, hoping that if enough people throw enough sand it will eventually come crashing down, but self-assured that you're going to keep throwing sand either way, win or lose.

Sure it's hard. Sure it entails a lot of disappointments and losses. But at least it's real. At least it stands a chance at beating the bastards, however small. As weak and pathetic as you can feel throwing haymakers at a globe-spanning empire some days, it sure beats the hell out of collaborating with it. And that's exactly what you'd be doing by joining up with fraudulent political factions which claim to oppose the empire.

Featured images via Wikimedia Commons.

Zionism Is Strangling Free Speech In Australia

A Palestinian-Australian man has been criminally charged for voicing criticisms of Zionism during a protest against Israel's genocide in Gaza. He could spend months in prison.

The Age reports that restaurant owner Hash Tayeh has been charged with four counts of "using insulting words in public" for repeatedly uttering the phrase "all Zionists are terrorists" at a pro-Palestine rally in Melbourne last year. According the The Age's Chris Vedelago, the punishment for this crime of political speech is "up to two months in prison for a first offence and six months for three or more offences."

"It is believed to be the first time that potential political speech has been deemed a criminal offence that breached the 'insulting' law," Vedelago reports, adding, "The charges are normally levied for using abusive or obscene language against police officers."

You really couldn't ask for a better illustration of the authoritarian dystopia that Australia has become than a news report about a man getting criminally charged for normal political speech with a law that is normally used to jail people who speak impolitely to the police.

These charges for speech crimes against Zionism follow a controversial assertion made last year by Australia's attorney-general Mark Dreyfus:

"The label Zionist is used, not in any way, accurately. When critics use that word, they actually mean Jew. They're not really saying Zionist, they're saying Jew because they know that they cannot say Jew, so they say Zionist or words [such as] Zeo or Zio."

Dreyfus might want to have a chat with outgoing Canadian prime minister Justin Trudeau, who just made headlines by proudly proclaiming "I am a Zionist" at his final press conference on Thursday.

Trudeau is not Jewish, nor is genocidal war criminal Joe Biden, who is on record saying on numerous occasions some variation of "I'm a Zionist. You don't have to be a Jew to be a Zionist."

Not all Jews are Zionists, and most Zionists are not Jewish. Zionism is a political ideology which upholds the western decision to drop an abusive apartheid ethnostate on top of a pre-existing civilization in historic Palestine and defend it by any amount of violence and tyranny necessary, and the majority of the people you see defending this status quo are westerners with no connection to the Jewish faith. The cult of Christian Zionism alone outnumbers the world's Jewish population by about two to one.

It is therefore wildly incorrect to conflate Zionism with Judaism, and it is also highly immoral. People who do this are assigning all Jews the blame for Israel's abuses, when the blame actually lies with the state of Israel and its western backers. As much as Israel apologists shriek and moan about "antisemitism" when they really mean supporting Palestinians, the real antisemitism problem in our society is the way our ruling institutions keep lumping all Jews in with the abuses of a genocidal apartheid state and the western empire which supports it.

That's all the imaginary "antisemitism" crisis is, in reality: people conflating anti-Zionism with antisemitism. If you declare that anti-Zionism is antisemitism and then Zionism starts butchering children by the tens of thousands in a genocidal onslaught, you are naturally going to see a rapid rise in "antisemitism" as you have defined it. It's a fallacious narrative used to justify the strangulation of political speech we are seeing today.

We're seeing that strangulation surge ahead in Australia with the McCarthyite witch hunt against pro-Palestinian voices, and in a decision by Australian universities to espouse a definition of "antisemitism" which is so speech-suppressing that it has been denounced by Amnesty International.

We are also seeing Zionism strangling free speech throughout the western world. German police are routinely assaulting pro-Palestine demonstrators. Pro-Palestinian journalists are being persecuted with increasing aggression in the UK and throughout Europe. In the US the Trump administration is working to stomp out pro-Palestine protests on university campuses while using AI to compile lists of people suspected of expressing support for Hamas on social media.

Almost every day we're seeing some new escalation in the western empire's efforts to stomp out speech that is critical of Israel. Westerners need to understand that we have moved far beyond the point where Israel is a threat only to middle eastern lives: it's a threat to us all, because the western governments who support it are stomping out our basic freedoms with increasing aggression in order to silence all criticisms of its abuses.

Even if you didn't have enough compassion to oppose Israel and its western backers because of their genocidal atrocities in the middle east, at this point you need to start opposing them out of sheer self-preservation. This isn't just about foreigners overseas anymore: it's about you. Your rights. Your freedom to voice your political opinions.

Zionism is a threat to civil rights everywhere. Zionism threatens us all.

Featured image via Adobe Stock.

Even More Assaults On Free Speech To Silence Criticism Of Israel
•Notes From The Edge Of The Narrative Matrix•

Acting on orders from the White House, immigration agents have arrested a Columbia University graduate for deportation due to his leadership of campus protests against Israel's genocidal atrocities in Gaza last year.

Palestinian activist Mahmoud Khalil is reportedly married to an American citizen and had had permanent residency in the US, but his green card has been revoked by the State Department as the Trump administration works to deport everyone they can possibly get away with deporting for criticizing Israel.

This is the equivalent of the Australian government revoking the permanent residency of my American husband Tim and deporting him because of our work criticizing the Gaza holocaust. The suffering that can be unleashed by a policy like this in the United States is hard to fathom.

This comes as we learn that the US government will be using AI to compile lists of people suspected of expressing support for Hamas on social media, and as the Trump administration announces that funding will be killed for any schools which allow "illegal protests" in support of Palestinians on their campuses.

I have said it before and I will say it again: there is no greater threat to free speech in our society than Israel and the western governments who support it. Civil rights are being stomped out throughout the western world to shut down all criticism of Israel.

We're now seeing escalations in western Zionism's assault on civil rights on a daily basis. Pretty much every day I'm reading about at least one western government silencing criticism of Israel with some new authoritarian abuse. Zionism is the number one threat to free speech in our society.

Westerners need to understand that Israel and the west's support for it are a direct threat to our personal freedom. This is about YOU now. If you didn't have enough compassion to oppose Israel for its genocidal atrocities, you should at least now oppose it to protect yourself.

•

Trump supporters are falling all over themselves trying to justify Trump's assaults on free speech the same way Bush supporters fell all over themselves to justify the authoritarianism of the Bush administration. Republicans haven't changed. They think they have but they haven't.

•

This happens as opposition to Israel becomes more urgently needed than ever. Israel has cut off all electricity to Gaza, which is expected to cripple Gaza's water supply by killing power to critical desalination plants. Once again this genocidal apartheid state is targeting civilians with deadly force in order to advance its depraved agendas, but anyone who wants to criticize such things is being aggressively targeted by increasingly tyrannical measures throughout the western world.

•

The most horrifying thing about all the footage of HTS thugs massacring people in Syria is not the violence itself, it's how happy its perpetrators are in the videos. Grinning. Laughing. Joking. It's deeply disturbing how easily people can be turned into monsters.

I've been on the receiving end of shrieking vitriol ever since I started this gig for opposing the western empire's regime change operations in Syria. Got a good dose of it last December when the operation finally succeeded. Now look. Look where it landed.

Always oppose the empire.

•

There's a video going around of young British men at some kind of pro-Ukraine event advocating sending British troops to Ukraine, and when the interviewer asks them if they themselves would volunteer to go put their own boots on the ground they act shocked and start stammering about how they're conscientious objectors and are not physically fit enough.

It's fascinating how often you'll see this sort of response from western armchair proxy warriors when you suggest that they should go and fight in this military intervention they're so keen on perpetuating. They often cannot seem to comprehend why anyone would think it's a compelling point that they are pushing the continuation of a war that they themselves would never agree to fight in, which is just so very revealing. It shows that they see the idea of other people fighting and dying in a war as a completely different and unrelated category to the idea of themselves fighting and dying in a war.

It shows that they don't view the people who fight in wars as fully human, with dreams and fears and families just like they have, who don't want to die a violent death any more than they do. It's genuinely never occurred to them to put themselves in the shoes of the people who are fighting and dying and getting their limbs blown off, and to think about what it would be like if the same thing were happening to them.

It's like a video game to these people. They don't see it as real in the same way their own lives are real. A war is something they watch unfold on social media and cheer and boo like a sporting event, not something involving real people who are just as capable of suffering and loss as they are.

A majority of Ukrainians now oppose the war and want a negotiated settlement as quickly as possible. If you want this horrific war to continue and yet you are not on front lines serving in the Foreign Legion, then you should definitely shut the fuck up. If you want Ukrainians to keep throwing their lives into a war against their will when you yourself are unwilling to do the same, then you have failed to mature as a human being on this planet. You lack a functioning empathy center in your brain, and it's a major character flaw, and you should go fix it.

Featured image via Adobe Stock.

It's not a free speech issue Mahmoud Khalil is a terrorist supporter and he's not even a citizen he has no right to make Jews feel afraid on campus with pro-Hamas demonstrations how dare you question our president while he deports terrorist scum we need our government to protect our ears from unauthorized speech and protect our minds from forbidden information the government is our friend antisemitism antisemitism antisemitism antisemitism Hamas Hamas Hamas Hamas terrorist terrorist terrorist terrorist MAGA MAGA MAGA MAGA MIGA MIGA MIGA MIGA

People Who Defend Trump's Assault On Free Speech Are Mindless Sheep

President Trump has taken to social media to boast about his administration's arrest of Palestinian activist Mahmoud Khalil for leading Columbia University campus demonstrations against Israel's genocidal atrocities in Gaza, proclaiming that "This is the first arrest of many to come."

"We know there are more students at Columbia and other Universities across the Country who have engaged in pro-terrorist, anti-Semitic, anti-American activity, and the Trump Administration will not tolerate it," Trump said.

And judging from what I'm seeing online, and the responses I've been getting to my criticisms of these abuses, most Trump supporters seem perfectly fine with these measures. Many are actively defending them.

Words can't express how disgusted I am with Trump supporters who defend their president stomping out speech rights for Israel after spending years wailing about the loss of free speech in America. It's beyond mere political differences. I don't respect them as people.

Of all the pathetic, groveling, bootlicking positions anyone could possibly espouse, it's hard to imagine one more egregious than twisting yourself into cognitive knots trying to find ways to excuse a president crushing free speech in your country to advance the interests of a foreign state after spending years yelling "America First" and whining about freedom of speech, just because that President happens to be a Republican.

If you are doing this, you're just admitting that you don't stand for anything, and you're just drifting along with the herd and supporting whatever the man in charge tells you to support. You're unthinking human livestock. A mindless, useless, pointless NPC. You have wasted all of your time on this planet, because you did not use that time to mature into a sovereign adult with basic intellectual agency and integrity.

Republicans have this adorable story about themselves where they believe they have changed since the George W Bush administration, but that's not what I'm seeing on social media today. I'm seeing the same shitbrained, power-worshipping sheep who cheered on every authoritarian abuse rolled out by the Bush administration. That's all this so-called "populist" movement calling itself "MAGA" turned out to be: all the same authoritarian bootlicking, but with more presents for Israel.

I saw a tweet from Michael Tracey the other day, "GOP free speech: You can say 'retarded' again, but you can't protest Israel."

That's the long and short of it, right there. When Trump supporters spent all those years yelling about the First Amendment, it turns out they weren't talking about the need to stop the powerful from silencing inconvenient political speech — they just wanted to be allowed to say "retard" and "tranny" on social media. As long as they get those completely irrelevant concessions from the powerful, they'll happily let their government set all kinds of speech-suppressing legal precedents, because they don't actually have any values or positions which pose any kind of challenge to the powerful. They're George W Bush Republicans LARPing as populist revolutionaries.

Someone who actually supports free speech says "I may not agree with what you say, but I will defend to the death your right to say it." Trump supporters say "I may not agree with what you say, but I'll defend to the death my government's right to silence you as long as a Republican is in office."

Worthless, spineless cucks. What an undignified way to live.

•

We Are Duped Into Blaming Our Problems On Everyone Except Our Rulers

Muslims are not a threat to you.

Russia is not a threat to you.

China is not a threat to you.

Trans people are not a threat to you.

Immigrants are not a threat to you.

If you find yourself resisting anything I just said, that's where they hooked you. That's where your rulers duped you into blaming your problems on something other than them.

You will notice that I am not saying there are no enemies and nobody poses a threat to us; there absolutely are, and they absolutely do. It's just that people are tricked and manipulated away from seeing the real enemies and the real threats where they are.

What poses a threat to you is the political status quo which robs your country of riches and resources to inflict military violence on innocent people overseas while strangling your civil rights and poisoning your planet. What poses a threat to you are the oligarchs and empire managers who uphold this status quo which is driving our species to authoritarian dystopia and extinction via environmental disaster or nuclear annihilation.

They want you blaming your problems on anyone else besides the actual source of your problems. They prefer to get you freaking out about their primary targets — the disobedient groups and nations they want to destroy to advance the interests of the empire — but if they can't accomplish that then they're happy to get you hating powerless groups who pose no real threat to you. Anything they can do to keep your eyes off your real oppressors: the billionaires, bankers, media barons, intelligence agencies, warmongers, ecocidal capitalists, military-industrial complex plutocrats, and all the empire lackeys in your official elected government.

They want us fighting each other, but we only pose a threat to each other if we buy into their bogus narratives of hostility and division. An immigrant is only threatened by a right winger because the right winger has been successfully duped into blaming his problems on the immigrant, and therefore elects empire lackeys who will make the immigrant's life more difficult. But without that artificially manufactured enmity, it's just two people being abused by the same pricks at the top.

Whenever I say stuff like this I'll get people voicing objections like "No no Caitlin you don't understand, we really truly ARE seriously dangerously threatened by The Trans Agenda" or whatever. But you're not. That's just you doing the thing I'm describing here. You're just buying into the exact scam I'm talking about. You're allowing your crosshairs to be moved from your oppressors to some irrelevant diversion in order to protect your oppressors.

At some point we need to stop falling for the scam. We need to wake up to the fact that we're all just a bunch of normal people living in a highly abusive society, and that our abusers are benefiting immensely from our inability to see through their divide-and-conquer manipulations and unite against them.

Muslims are not a threat to you.

Russia is not a threat to you.

China is not a threat to you.

Trans people are not a threat to you.

Immigrants are not a threat to you.

The US empire is a threat to you.

Your own government is a threat to you.

Oligarchs are a threat to you.

Nuclear brinkmanship is a threat to you.

Ecocide is a threat to you.

War and militarism are a threat to you.

Tyranny is a threat to you.

Propaganda is a threat to you.

Your enemies are not in Moscow, Beijing and Tehran. Your enemies are in Washington, Virginia, New York and Los Angeles. Your enemies are in London, Paris, Brussels and Tel Aviv.

Your abusers are not some far away nation your own government doesn't like, nor are they some marginalized group your government doesn't care about. Your abusers are your government itself, and all its allies and assets around the world, and the network of oligarchs and empire managers who call the shots in this globe-spanning power structure from behind the scenes.

The sooner we get this straight, the sooner we can sort out all these problems we're currently being duped into blaming on the wrong people.

Featured image via Adobe Stock.

Trump Is Bombing Yemen For Israel
•Notes From The Edge Of The Narrative Matrix•

*The US is bombing Yemen again after Houthi leaders
announced that their blockade on Israeli shipping would resume
due to Israel's siege on Gaza.*

Trump could have used Washington's immense leverage over Israel to force Netanyahu to honor the ceasefire agreement and allow aid into Gaza. Instead he let the IDF lay siege to Gaza and started bombing Yemen for Israel, because he's a warmongering Israel cuck.

Trump is bombing Yemen for Israel, rushing weapons to Israel despite its flagrant ceasefire violations, and rolling out authoritarian measure after authoritarian measure to stop Americans from criticizing Israel. Because that's what you get when you vote for America First.

Do you want to know how much of a pathetic Israel lackey Trump is? Earlier this month his nominated hostage envoy Adam Boehler went on CNN and proclaimed that the United States is "not an agent of Israel". Days later, the White House withdrew Boehler's nomination.

•

Known things:

1. Trump is a servant of Israel.

2. Trump is on the Epstein flight logs.

3. Epstein worked with Israeli intelligence.

4. Epstein was running a sexual blackmail operation.

5. Trump is obstructing the release of the Epstein files.

Question:

Exactly how many kids did Trump rape?

•

It's cool how Republicans are finally dropping that phony "We're populists fighting the Deep State" schtick and returning to their authentic "Anyone who opposes authoritarianism loves terrorists, let's fight more wars in the middle east" roots.

Trump supporters would wipe their asses with the US Constitution and deport their own mothers if doing so would help their government send one more 2000-pound bomb to Israel.

•

The other day I shared a report about Israel continuing its insanely evil practice of murdering children in Gaza with sniper drones, and I got multiple people in my replies commenting "Release the hostages!" as a response.

Israel supporters are the worst people in the world.

•

I have no sympathy for Israelis, nor for Israel supporters who say they "feel unsafe". This isn't because I am uncaring, it's because I know any sympathy I might point in that direction will be harnessed and used to murder Palestinians, start wars, and destroy free speech rights.

•

When you proclaim that anti-Zionism is antisemitism and then Zionism murders tens of thousands of children, you are naturally going to see a rise in "antisemitism" as you have defined it. That's all this whole "antisemitism crisis" narrative has been from the very beginning.

Zionism is not a religion, it's a fucking political ideology. It's always legitimate to criticize a political ideology. Saying it's evil forbidden speech to express disdain for Zionism is the same as saying it's evil forbidden speech to express disdain for white nationalism. Zionism is the political ideology which supports the west's decision to drop an apartheid ethnostate on top of a pre-existing population and maintain that apartheid ethnostate by any amount of violence and abuse necessary.

You can't butcher children by the tens of thousands with the backing of the most powerful war machine on the planet in the name of supporting this political ideology and then legitimately cry victim when people have something to say about it. That's not a thing.

•

People tend to bluff the opposite of whatever hand they're holding; newbies do it in poker, and everyone does it with their ego. Conservatives are afraid of everything, so they posture as hypermasculine tough guys. Liberals are bootlickers who act like heroes of social justice.

You see this dynamic everywhere, on the personal level as well as political. The person who feels small acts big. The person who feels dumb acts like a know it all. You see some bloke acting like he's better than everyone else and think "That guy needs to be brought down a few pegs," but really he's only doing that because he feels inferior to everybody; you can't bring him down any lower than he's already brought himself. They're all just bluffing the opposite of the hand they believe they've been dealt.

Featured image via Trump White House (Public Domain).

Israel Lied About Murdered Children To Justify Murdering Children

Israel resumed its genocidal campaign of annihilation in Gaza early Tuesday morning, killing hundreds in a matter of hours, including many children. As of this writing, the death toll from this assault is reportedly at least 413.

Israel is not even pretending that Hamas violated the ceasefire agreement it signed on to in January, saying instead that the decision to resume the onslaught was made because Hamas had been rejecting a significantly altered new agreement put forward by the Trump administration which would have allowed Israel to postpone moving toward a lasting peace.

"This follows Hamas's repeated refusal to release our hostages, as well as its rejection of all of the proposals it has received from US Presidential Envoy Steve Witkoff and from the mediators," reads a statement from Israeli Prime Minister Benjamin Netanyahu.

"Israel will, from now on, act against Hamas with increasing military strength," Netanyahu said.

Of course we all know Israel is not really acting against Hamas; Israel is acting against the entire population of the Gaza Strip. The plan to eliminate all Palestinians in Gaza has been openly confessed to by the president of the United States, who went as far as posting a freakishly disturbing AI-generated music video on social media about the future of Gaza after its US-backed ethnic cleansing. Israel is simply making the enclave as dangerous and uninhabitable as possible so that everyone who lives there will be forced to either leave or die.

And this was all planned in advance. As soon as the Gaza ceasefire agreement was announced, the Netanyahu-aligned pundits in Israeli media were already saying they knew for a fact that the prime minister wasn't going to allow the deal to move on to its second phase. After Netanyahu visited Washington and stayed for nearly a week, the Israeli outlet Haaretz reported that the prime minister was planning to sabotage the ceasefire deal upon his return. Now here we are, watching Netanyahu completely torch the ceasefire after weeks of actively sabotaging it.

Not only was this all planned in advance — it was also propagandized for in advance. Israel and the western political-media class spent days pushing the atrocity propaganda narrative that Hamas had murdered child hostages Kfir and Ariel Bibas in the early weeks of the Gaza onslaught — not just murdered them, but murdered them with their bare hands.

Public outrage was deliberately drummed up around this narrative, despite no evidence ever being presented to the public that it was true. Western landmarks like the Empire State Building and the Eiffel Tower were lit orange at night in a transparent attempt to highlight the children's whiteness for westerners who've been trained to ignore the deaths of darker middle eastern children. Israel supporters brayed for Palestinian blood as this babies-on-bayonets atrocity propaganda was pushed into their minds to manufacture consent for future atrocities.

And it was all a psyop. Zeteo's Muhammad Shehada reported a month and a half ago — weeks before the Bibas narrative was unfurled — that Israel's narrative managers appeared to be gearing up to use the Bibas kids to justify future bloodshed by pretending they didn't know whether the children were alive or not, swearing vengeance if they were dead. Hamas reported back in November 2023 that the Bibas children had been killed in an Israeli airstrike along with their mother. In December 2023 it was reported in the mainstream press that Hamas had offered to return their bodies to Israel but Israel refused, telling the press that "Israel will not address propaganda-based reports coming from Hamas".

Lo and behold, the atrocity propaganda narrative about the Bibas children was rolled out a few weeks later when their bodies were returned by Hamas as part of the ceasefire agreement, just as Shehada

had anticipated. And just last week, former Israeli defense minister Yoav Gallant admitted publicly that he had known the Bibas kids were dead the entire time, directly contradicting the feigned shock of Israel and its spinmeisters when the bodies of the children were returned.

To this day, Israel has presented the public with no evidence of any kind that the Bibas siblings were murdered by the bare hands of their captors, rather than by the same Israeli airstrikes that were killing women and children every day in the same area as common sense would suggest. Given Israel's extensive history of lying about exactly this sort of thing, we can safely assume that the evidence was never presented because there isn't any evidence.

They lied. They lied about murdered children in order to justify murdering children, just like they lied about beheaded babies on October 7 in order to justify killing thousands of babies in Gaza.

When it comes to Israel, every accusation is a confession.

Featured image is a screenshot from the Prime Minister of Israel on X.

This Is Trump's Genocide Now
•Notes From The Edge Of The Narrative Matrix•

This is Trump's genocide. Trump is just as culpable for what happens in Gaza as Netanyahu. Just as guilty as Biden was during the last administration.

Trump signed off on the reignition of the Gaza holocaust. He spent weeks sabotaging the ceasefire and then gave the thumbs up to the resumption of the genocide. He did this while bombing Yemen and threatening war with Iran for Israel.

I don't know why Trump has done these things. Maybe it's all for the Adelson cash. Maybe Epstein recorded him doing something unsavory with a minor during their long association and gave it to Israeli intelligence for blackmail purposes. Maybe he owed somebody a favor for bailing him out of his business failures in the past. Maybe he's just a psychopath who enjoys murdering children. I don't know, and it doesn't really matter. What matters is that he did it, and he is responsible for his actions.

Trump supporters will justify literally anything their president does using whatever excuses they need to, but they are only revealing how completely empty and unprincipled their political faction is. They are unthinking worshippers of power who go along with whatever the president tells them to. By continuing to support Trump even as he continues Biden's legacy of mass murder in the middle east, they are proving themselves to be mindless stormtroopers for the empire in full view of the entire world.

You can still support Trump if you hate immigrants and LGBTQ people and want lower taxes for the obscenely wealthy, but there is no legitimate reason to support him on antiwar or anti-establishment grounds. He's just another evil Republican mass murderer president.

•

Republicans in 2002: We need more authoritarianism and more wars in the middle east. Anyone who disagrees is a terrorist supporter.

Republicans in 2025: We need more authoritarianism and more wars in the middle east. Anyone who disagrees is a terrorist supporter, and antisemite.

•

By the way has anyone checked on the western Zionist Jews? How are their feelings feeling today? Are they feeling nice feelings or bad feelings? Are their feelings feeling safe or unsafe? We need wall to wall news coverage of this supremely urgent issue; no time to cover any other story.

•

I write so much about the fake "antisemitism crisis" not only because it's being used to destroy civil rights throughout the western world, but because it's one of the most dark and disturbing things I've ever witnessed.

It's been so intensely creepy watching all of western society mobilize around a complete and utter fiction in order to stomp out all criticism of a foreign state. It's about as dystopian a thing as you can possibly imagine, all these pundits and politicians pretending to believe that Jewish safety is seriously being threatened by an epidemic of antisemitism which must be aggressively silenced by any means necessary. All to shut down opposition to the worst inclinations of a genocidal apartheid state and the complicity of our own western governments with its crimes.

And we're all expected to treat this scam seriously. Anyone who says the emperor has no clothes and calls this mass deception what it is gets tarred with the "antisemite" label and treated as further evidence that we're all a hair's breadth from seeing Jews rounded up onto trains again if we don't all hurry up and shut down anti-genocide protests on university campuses. They're not just acting out a fraudulent melodrama staged to rob us of our rights, they're demanding that we participate in it by pretending it's not what it plainly is.

It's not just tyranny, it's tyranny that orders people to clap along with it. It's such a disgusting, evil thing to do to people. Such psychologically dominating abusive behavior. The more you look at it, the creepier it gets.

•

The anti-imperialist left is what MAGA and right wing "populism" pretend to be. We ACTUALLY oppose the empire's warmongering — not only when Democrats are in power. We ACTUALLY want to defeat the deep state — we don't applaud billionaire Pentagon contractors like Elon Musk taking power. We ACTUALLY oppose the establishment order — because the establishment order is capitalist. We ACTUALLY stand up to the powerful — we don't offload half the blame onto immigrants and marginalized groups.

The anti-imperialist left is also what liberals pretend to be. We ACTUALLY support the working class. We ACTUALLY stand up for the little guy. We ACTUALLY want justice and equality. We ACTUALLY support civil rights. We ACTUALLY oppose tyranny.

Everything the human heart longs for lies in the death of capitalism, militarism and empire, and yet both of the dominant western political factions of our day support continuing all of these things. This is because westerners spend their entire lives marinating in power-serving propaganda which herds them into these two mainstream political factions to ensure that they will pose no meaningful challenges to our rulers. All political energy is funneled into movements and parties which are set up to maintain the status quo while pretending to support the people, with the illusion of political freedom sustained by a false two-party dichotomy in which both factions serve the same ruling power structure.

Of course, what mainstream liberalism and right wing "populism" have to offer that anti-imperialist socialism does not is the ability to win major elections with successful candidates. This is because generations of imperial psyops have gone into stomping out the anti-imperialist left in the western world, and because only candidates which uphold the status quo are ever allowed to get close to winning an election. This doesn't mean mainstream liberalism or right wing "populism" are the answer, it just means our prison warden isn't going to hand us the keys to the exit door.

At some point we're going to have to rise up and use the power of our numbers to force the urgently needed changes we long to see in our world. Everything in our society is set up to prevent this from ever happening. That's all the two mainstream political factions are designed to do. That's why they both have phony "populist" elements within them which purport to be leading a brave revolutionary charge against the establishment, while herding everyone into support for the two status quo political parties. And that's why the anti-imperialist left is everything they pretend to be.

Featured image via Gage Skidmore (CC BY-SA 2.0)

of defence, Israel Katz

Citizens of Gaza, this is your last warning

Israel Makes Its Most Explicit Statement Of Genocidal Intent Yet

Israeli Defense Minister Israel Katz has published an explicit statement of genocidal intent toward the people of Gaza, threatening civilians in the enclave with collective punishment in the form of "total devastation" if they do not find a way to overthrow Hamas and free all Israeli hostages.

Katz's statement reads as follows:

"Residents of Gaza, this is your final warning. The first Sinwar destroyed Gaza, and the second Sinwar will bring upon it total ruin. The Israeli Air Force's attack against Hamas terrorists was only the first step. What follows will be far harsher, and you will bear the full cost.

"Evacuation of the population from combat zones will soon resume. If all Israeli hostages are not released and Hamas is not kicked out of Gaza, Israel will act with force you have not known before.

"Take the advice of the U.S. President: return the hostages and kick out Hamas, and new options will open up for you — including relocation to other parts of the world for those who choose. The alternative is destruction and total devastation."

When Katz says "Take the advice of the US president," he is referring to a statement made by President Trump earlier this month which made essentially the same threat addressed "to the People of Gaza," saying, "A beautiful Future awaits, but not if you hold Hostages. If you do, you are DEAD! Make a SMART decision. RELEASE THE HOSTAGES NOW, OR THERE WILL BE HELL TO PAY LATER!"

When I criticized the US president for these remarks which explicitly threaten Gaza's civilians, I got a deluge of Trump supporters telling me he wasn't really talking about "the people of Gaza" as he said, but

was rather speaking only about the ones who are actively holding hostages. Katz's statement makes it abundantly clear that they were wrong, and that those of us who called a spade a spade at the time were correct.

The Israeli defense minister is simply following Trump's position and reiterating what everyone who isn't a blinkered partisan hack knew Trump was saying two weeks ago. He is doing this in exactly the same way Benjamin Netanyahu followed Trump's position on ethnically cleansing Gaza last month by enthusiastically endorsing the plan Trump put forward to permanently remove all Palestinians from the enclave. Trump puts forward the plan, and Israeli officials put it into action.

So you've got both the US and Israeli governments openly threatening the entire population of the Gaza strip with the war crime of collective punishment if they don't somehow kick Hamas out of Gaza, and additionally announcing the intent to inflict "total devastation" upon that population if they do not.

This is about as explicit an admission of genocidal intent as you can possibly come up with.

In its genocide case against Israel in the International Court of Justice, South African prosecutors compiled a mountain of evidence of Israeli officials announcing the intent to commit genocide in Gaza, such as Netanyahu describing Gaza's population as "Amalek" in reference to a Bible story about a people who were completely annihilated on the orders of God, or former Israeli defense minister Yoav Gallant

describing Palestinians in Gaza as "human animals" while declaring a "total siege" on the enclave.

Al Jazeera's Raz Segal and Penny Green wrote the following regarding the ICJ case last year:

"The crime of genocide has two elements — intention and execution — both of which have to be proven when accusations are made... Intention is usually harder to prove when accusations of genocide are made; the petitioner has to be able to prove "intent to destroy, in whole or in part, a national, ethnical, racial or religious group, as such," in the language of the UN Convention on the Prevention and Punishment of the Crime of Genocide. But in Israel's case, intention too has been laid bare by an ample amount of evidence — as the South African legal team pointed out."

And Katz's statement is probably the most clear and explicit admission yet. It's hard to imagine a clearer declaration of genocidal intent than delivering a video statement addressed to a civilian population threatening them with "total devastation" if they don't do as they're told.

We may be sure that these statements by Katz and Trump have been added to files held by those who hope to successfully prosecute these monsters for war crimes one day. We may also be sure that they will be recorded in what will eventually be seen as one of the darker chapters in our civilization's history.

Featured image is a screenshot from Israel Katz on X.

Trump Is Just Bush In A Red Hat
•Notes From The Edge Of The Narrative Matrix•

Trump is butchering children in Gaza, stomping out free speech in the US, bombing Yemen for Israel, and preparing for full-scale war with Iran in plans which reportedly include the possible use of nuclear weapons.

And from what I can see, Trump supporters are mostly fine with it. Everything the so-called MAGA movement claims to stand for is a lie.

"MAGA" is just Republicans doing Republican things. Ten years ago the GOP started wallpapering over its shattered reputation from the Bush administration with a right wing populist message which purported to oppose neoconservative war agendas, support free speech, seek to drain the swamp, and put America first. In practice what we are seeing is Trump murdering and warmongering in the middle east just like Bush, rolling out freakish authoritarian agendas in the US just like Bush, advancing longstanding neoconservative agendas just like Bush, and putting Israel first just like every Republican for decades.

Trump is all the most evil things Bush was, but MAGA morons pretend he's something different because he put on a red hat. Dumbest, most pathetic and fraudulent political faction in existence.

•

As footage of dead kids in Gaza fills your social media timeline once again, keep in mind that the reason the empire has worked so hard to stomp out all criticism of Israel's western-backed atrocities is because our rulers planned on sponsoring a lot more atrocities and murdering a lot more kids.

•

Ever trip on how Israel and its western backers keep calling this a "war"? What's happening in Gaza is not a war, it's a few thousand guys with homemade rockets fighting an entire empire, and Israel isn't even focused on them — it's focused on the entire population of Gaza.

States often try to avoid using the word "war" to describe their actions due to people's negative associations with it. The US likes to call its wars "humanitarian interventions". Russia called its invasion of Ukraine a "Special Military Operation". But Israel immediately rushed in to call its naked ethnic cleansing operation in Gaza a "war", as did its western allies and their propaganda press. Why is that?

I will tell you why. It's to justify permanently taking Gaza away from the Palestinians. Israel has an established track record of using the wars it has fought to grab up more territory, which its apologists then justify by saying things like "Yeah well they lost a war in 1967, you lose territory when you fight a war and lose." They're laying the narrative foundation to make sure everyone in the future will see Gaza in the same light after they annex it, purge it of Palestinians, and replace them with Jews.

That's all this has ever been: not a war with Hamas, but another Israeli land grab. There are mountains of evidence that Israeli officials let October 7 happen on purpose in order to justify this land grab, and they've been framing this as a "war" ever since to make sure they can get away with it.

Framing this as a war has other benefits to be sure, such as framing the civilians and civilian infrastructure it has been deliberately targeting as "collateral damage" instead of systematic extermination and demolition. But first and foremost this is about the expansion of Israeli territory.

A new Economist/YouGov poll has found that most Republicans believe protesting your government should be legal—except for protests against Israel. When it comes to protesting Israel a majority of Republicans either believe it should be illegal or are not sure.

I don't even know what to say to this. Imagine being someone answering those polling questions and not taking your own answers as a call to do some serious self-reflection. Imagine coming right out and admitting something like this about yourself, and then not changing.

•

It's the people going "HAHA GAZA'S ON FIRE I BET YOU WISH YOU'D VOTED FOR KAMALA NOW" who really get to me. This is exactly why the Democrats lost: because they saw Gaza as nothing more than a political plaything to be ignored when inconvenient and gloated about when convenient. This is just a game to these assholes.

These freaks spent months shouting down everyone who protested against the genocidal atrocities of Joe Biden and dismissing anyone who had a problem with Harris refusing to put any daylight between herself and the president on this extremely important issue. Now that Trump is continuing Biden's genocide they're somehow acting like they're on the right side of history? Fuck off you obnoxious shitstains.

Featured image via Gage Skidmore (CC BY-SA 2.0)

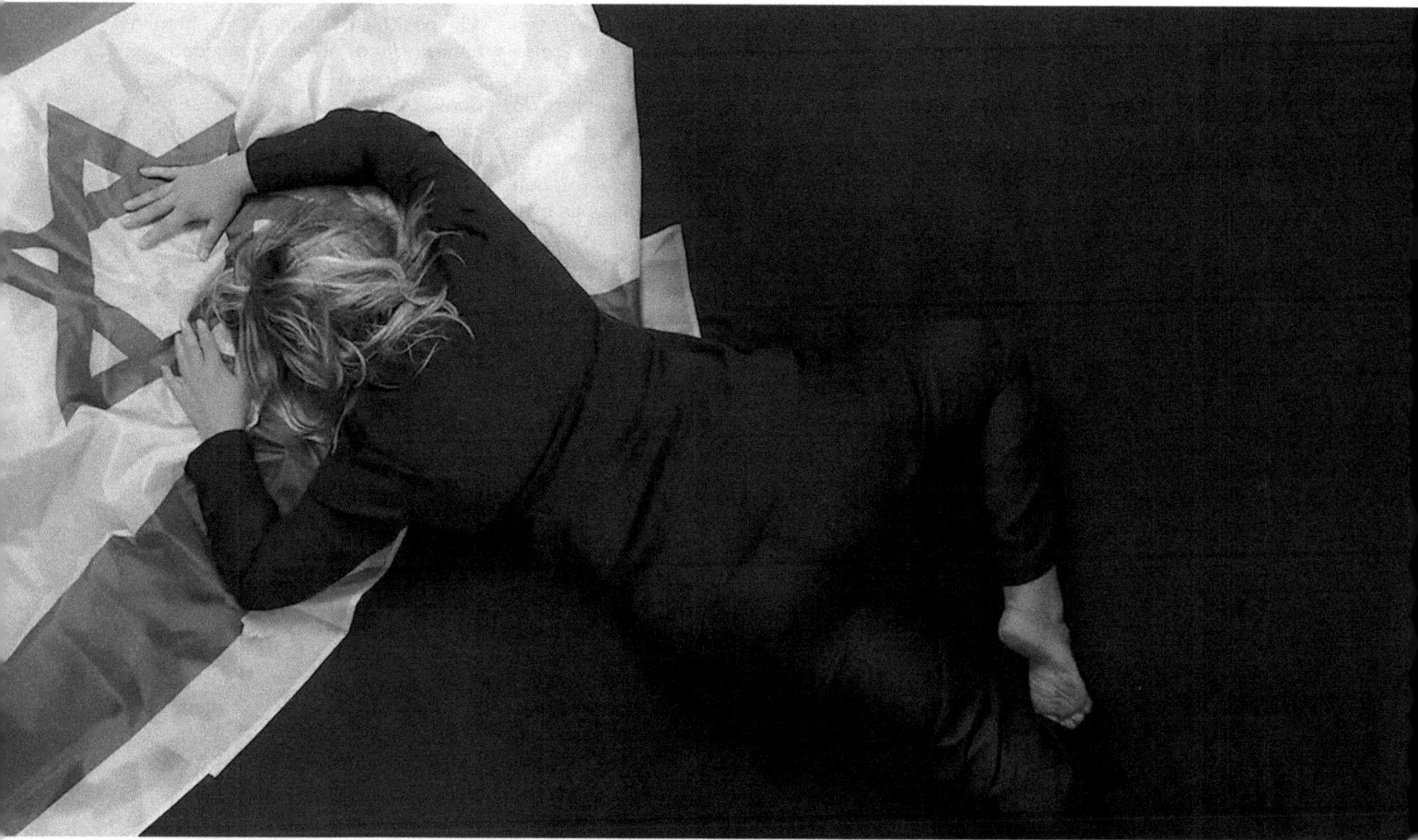

Israel Exists Simultaneously As The Perpetual Aggressor And The Perpetual Victim

One major challenge is that Zionists benefit from abusing Palestinians and exerting influence in western governments, and they **also** *benefit from people opposing these things — because it can be used to feed their victim-LARPing "antisemitism" narrative.*

This dynamic allows Israel to go all-out in committing mass atrocities and apartheid abuses while Zionist oligarchs like Miriam Adelson openly purchase western governments without having to worry about the damage it does to their public image, because any response to the damage it does to their public image can be reframed as "antisemitism" and used to advance their interests even further by stomping out civil rights.

People demonstrate against Israel's genocidal atrocities? That's antisemitism — those protesters need to be silenced, arrested, and deported. People object to blatant Zionist influence in their governments? Antisemitic conspiracy theories; we need more hate speech laws and internet censorship. Palestinians take up armed resistance against their oppressors? Israel is the victim of unprovoked attacks from Jew-hating Arabs.

Even real anti-Jewish prejudice benefits the Zionists, because it strengthens the narrative about an urgent crisis of antisemitism which must be crushed by any amount of force necessary, as well as the narrative that Jews need a nation of their own where they can feel safe. So Israel can openly mass murder children while Israeli officials make overt statements of genocidal intent, and if someone blames all Jews for this because they see a state committing atrocities under the banner of the Star of David while claiming to represent all Jews, it only benefits Israel and its supporters.

(As an aside, this is why it's so important not to blame this on "the Jews". It's not just that it's inaccurate — not all Jews are Zionists, the majority of Zionists are non-Jews, and some of the most effective anti-Zionists in the world happen to be Jewish — it's that you're doing exactly what the Zionists and the empire propagandists want you to do. You're doing their job for them. Don't be a pro bono Israel propagandist. Make them work for that shit.)

Zionism therefore benefits from abuse and influence, and also benefits from any backlash against its abuse and influence. It is able to do this because Israel is backed by the propaganda machine of the western empire — the most powerful weapon of mass psychological influence ever devised. If the western political-media class were not constantly running cover for Israel's crimes and helping Zionism spin all opposition to Israel as antisemitism, Israel would not be able to pull off this freakish cognitive straddle where it is simultaneously both the aggressor and the victim at all times.

And this is why it's so important to fight against the western empire's propaganda about Israel. Israel's reliance on the imperial propaganda machine is the only weak point in this otherwise unassailable dynamic where any backlash against Israel's abuses is harnessed and turned into a weapon to defend Israel. Propaganda only works if you don't know it's happening to you, so the only way to keep people from buying into the victim-LARPing of the Zionists is to open people's eyes to the truth.

Once enough people see with sufficient clarity the lies and manipulations which go into protecting the interests of this genocidal apartheid state, Israel loses one of its most powerful weapons, because nobody's going to buy into the narrative framework wherein Israel and its supporters try to frame themselves as the victims of the opposition to their abuses.

You fight against the propaganda by spreading truth and understanding about this dynamic in whatever way you can. Talk to people. Share useful information. Attend demonstrations. Distribute literature. Tweet, blog, make videos, make zines, make street art; whatever tools you have at your disposal to help people understand what's really going on with Israel and the western empire.

All positive changes in human behavior are always preceded by an expansion of consciousness. Consciousness and dysfunction cannot coexist. All we need to do to bring health to this world is to spread awareness of the truth, so that the dysfunction which can only survive in darkness is unable to sustain itself.

Featured image via Adobe Stock.

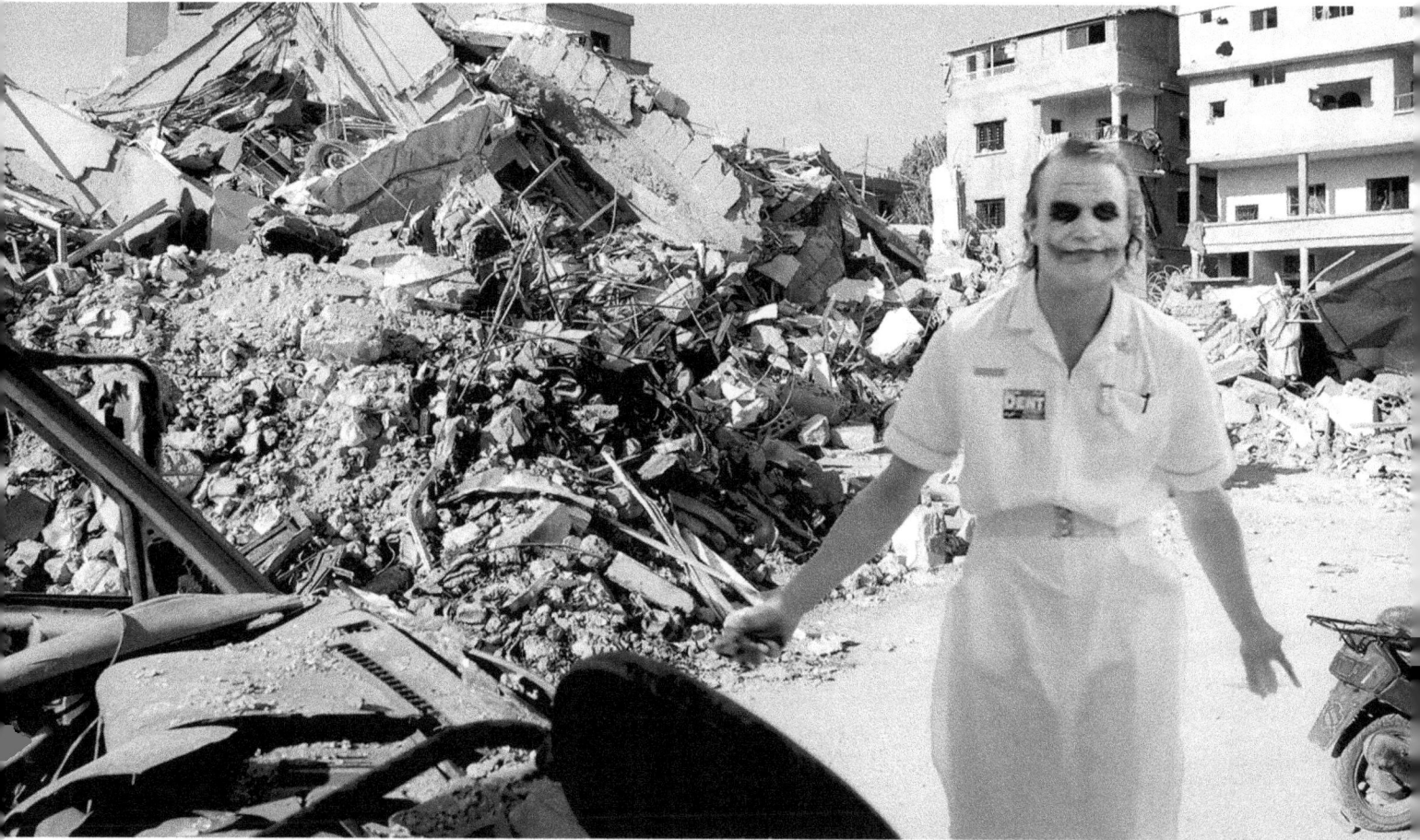

In Movies We Understand That The Genocidal Child Murderers Who Blow Up Hospitals Are The Villains

Remember in The Dark Knight when we all applauded the Joker for heroically blowing up a hospital?

Or remember when we watched Star Wars and cheered for the protagonist Darth Vader as he destroyed a planet to punish the rebel scum for daring to resist him?

How about when we watched Schindler's List anxiously hoping the Nazis would be able to thwart the diabolical scheming of the villain Oskar Schindler to prevent them from committing genocide?

Or when we watched Avatar and cheered for the interstellar megacorporation and its army of mercenaries to displace the indigenous people of Pandora to steal their land?

Or when we watched The Pelican Brief hoping the heroes would find some way to kill Julia Roberts and Denzel Washington to stop them from reporting the truth about their crimes?

Or when we watched The Pianist and wept at the evil Jews attacking innocent Nazis in the Warsaw Ghetto Uprising?

Or when we watched The Lord of the Rings and booed the villainous men, elves and dwarves fighting to survive a siege by Saruman's heroic army of orcs?

Or when we watched V for Vendetta on the edge of our seats worried that the government would fail to stomp out the rebellion, suppress the truth from coming out, and impose more authoritarian measures on the people?

Or when we watched Revenge of the Sith and cheered for the hero Anakin Skywalker mass murdering children in order to wipe the Jedi out of existence?

Yeah, I don't remember that either.

Nobody seems to have trouble figuring out who the real villains are when it's happening in the movies. The narrative managers and spinmeisters make it a lot harder to sort out the villains from the victims in real life.

Normally it's misguided to view any conflict as simply evil villains murdering innocent victims, but not with Israel and Gaza. It's an apartheid state that's backed by a globe-spanning empire, raining bombs onto a giant concentration camp packed full of children because they're the wrong ethnicity.

It's pretty black and white, actually.

Image via Masser for Wikimedia Commons, remixed by the author for commentary purposes.

Palestinians Didn't Choose The Religion Of Their Oppressors
•Notes From The Edge Of The Narrative Matrix•

One of the dumbest narratives we're asked to swallow about Palestinians is that they are guilty of anti-Jewish prejudice which makes them comparable to Nazis. Palestinians didn't choose the religion of their oppressors; any hatred they have toward Israelis is because Israelis are the ones oppressing and murdering them, not because of their religion. Expecting Palestinians not to hate the oppressors who hate them just because those oppressors happen to be Jewish is shitbrained thinking.

Every so often you'll see the IDF plant a copy of Mein Kampf in a building in Gaza and then wave it around as though it would somehow justify what Israel is doing to the Palestinians, and it's just so stupid. The reason we've come to abhor hatred toward Jews in the west is because we know the west has an extensive history of committing atrocities against Jewish people because of their religion.

Palestinians harbor no such prejudice and are guilty of no such crimes. Any violence they've inflicted upon Israelis has been in an effort to keep their land and resist tyrannical oppression, not because they have some weird European Hitlerite hatred toward Jews. Anytime you hear Palestinians talk about "the Jews" they're always talking solely and exclusively about their oppressors in the context of the occupation; they're not talking about some Jewish guy in Canada.

Palestinians would hate their oppressors whether the oppression was being inflicted by Hindus, Buddhists or Catholics. That's normal. That's how people's minds and emotions work; we hate people who hate us, and we hate people who abuse us. Any failure to understand this is a failure to put yourself in someone else's shoes and imagine what it would be like to live in their situation. It's a sign that you lack normal human empathy.

•

The world needs Israel. Without Israel where would sexual predators go for safety and protection? Where would we get our surveillance technology? Who would use human targets to field test new kinds of murder robots, military explosives and AI systems used to kill entire families?

•

Critics of Israel should familiarize themselves with Hitchens's razor: "What can be asserted without evidence can also be dismissed without evidence."

Whether it's beheaded babies, mass rapes, Hamas bases in hospitals, or Hamas killing the Bibas kids with their bare hands, if it's being asserted without evidence, it can be immediately dismissed.

•

It is a well-documented fact that Israel and its supporters use lobbying, campaign funding and blackmail to exert influence over western nations. It is also a fact that the US empire has the power to stop Israel from doing this at any time, but chooses not to. The empire managers in the official elected government don't do anything to stop these influence operations, nor do the empire managers in the far more powerful unelected national security state. Does anyone really believe Israel would still be exerting such massive influence over the US government if the CIA determined that this was impeding their agendas of global domination?

It follows that the Zionist influence operations exist because the empire wants them to. The artificially manufactured support for Israel has been deemed a necessary evil to help ensure constant violence, division and instability in the middle east and justify endless military presence in a crucial geostrategic region which, if left to its own devices, might unite and conduct its affairs in a way that is disadvantageous to western interests.

There are many other nations in the middle east who are aligned with the US and are used to advance its interests in the region, but none of them are fully dependent on support from the US government for their continued existence. It's a completely artificial construct that was inserted into the middle east like a glass shard into a foot, and its continued existence benefits both the settler colonialists who live there and the long-term hegemonic interests of the US-centralized empire.

I say all this to point out that the west isn't some passive innocent victim of manipulations by the big mean tyrant Israel. It is just as guilty of Israel's crimes as Israel itself, because those crimes are inseparable from the western empire as a whole. You see some on the right trying to argue that the west would be this wonderful virtuous place if not for the malign influence of those nasty Jews, but this narrative is refuted by the entire historical existence of the western world. The west has always been a warmongering, genocidal civilization driven by conquest and domination, and the western settler-colonialist project of Israel is just one more manifestation of the dystopia we are living in.

•

Defending Trump's warmongering in the middle east by babbling about his peacemaking efforts in Ukraine is the same as saying it's okay for him to torch Gaza because he's not bombing Argentina. It's nonsensical. You don't negate your crimes by being less criminal somewhere else.

•

Whenever I criticize Trump's actions in the middle east I'll get some Democrat going "I BET YOU WISH YOU'D SUPPORTED KAMALA NOW, HUH?"

That's not what this is, idiots. I did this exact same commentary throughout the Biden administration, because Biden is also evil. I am simply criticizing the world's most murderous and destructive power structure and whatever empire managers happen to be sitting at the front desk while it happens. This is just what it looks like when you apply scrutiny to the empire without being a partisan hack.

•

Bernie Sanders has been such a worthless empire simp I sometimes wonder why the Democratic Party establishment even bothered sabotaging his primary campaigns. They would have gotten another Obama, selling people false hope while advancing the interests of oligarchy and empire.

•

Our species evolved these brains of unprecedented sophistication only to use them to destroy our biosphere, invent new ways to blow each other up, and make ourselves miserable with our own thoughts.

•

It's not about hostages. It's not about Hamas. It's not about terrorism. Those aren't the reasons, they're the excuses. The excuses to expel Palestinians and turn more Palestinian land into Israeli land. That's all this has ever been about. Anyone who says otherwise is lying.

Featured image via Adobe Stock.

It's An Awkward Time To Be A Liberal Israel Supporter

Senate minority leader Chuck Schumer said in a recent interview that his job "is to keep the left pro-Israel," which is just sad. Being a liberal Israel supporter these days probably feels like being a defense attorney for an accused murderer who won't shut up about how much he loves murdering.

A Palestinian co-director of the Oscar-winning film No Other Land was assaulted and injured by a gang of Israeli settlers in the West Bank village of Susya before being abducted by Israeli soldiers on Monday. Hamdan Ballal and two other Palestinians were reportedly transferred from the Israeli military to the police for questioning, and as of this writing are still detained.

No Other Land is a documentary about Israeli abuses toward Palestinians in the occupied West Bank, which makes the lynch mob assault by the settlers not only ironic but completely vindicating of Ballal's work. These freaks are so consumed by hatred and Zionist brain rot that they actually thought they'd advance their cause by attacking Palestinians in the West Bank in response to a documentary about the mistreatment of Palestinians in the West Bank.

This happens as Israel adds two more bodies to the mountain of Palestinian journalists it has deliberately killed in Gaza. Al Jazeera reporter Hossam Shabat and Palestine Today TV correspondent Mohammad Mansour were both killed in separate airstrikes in different parts of the Gaza Strip on Monday, bringing the total number of Palestinian journalists killed in the Gaza holocaust to 208.

Israel is murdering journalists and persecuting documentary filmmakers because Israel hates truth. It kills press workers in Gaza for the same reason it blocks western reporters from entering the scorched Palestinian territory: because Israel doesn't want people to see the full picture of its atrocities.

This comes after Israeli Defense Minister Israel Katz made amazingly explicit statements of genocidal intent last week, telling the entire population of Gaza that they will face "total devastation" if they do not find some way to overthrow Hamas themselves and return all the hostages.

They're just getting more and more brazen with this stuff. More and more often, to a further and further extent, Israel is showing its true face to the world.

The other day Israel demolished Gaza's only specialized cancer treatment hospital and an adjacent medical school in its ongoing systematic destruction of the enclave's entire healthcare system with the goal of making it unlivable.

Shortly thereafter, Israel bombed another hospital in Khan Younis, killing a member of Hamas's political bureau as well as a 16 year-old boy. The imperial media fell all over themselves to churn out headlines announcing that Israel had targeted a Hamas leader in a strike on a hospital — as though bombing hospitals is this perfectly acceptable thing we should all view as normal now — but we all know these same media outlets would be shrieking their lungs out if any of the empire's enemies did this exact same thing.

As Jonathan Cook points out in a recent essay, this is the same as if Hamas had bombed the hospital Benjamin Netanyahu stayed at earlier this year in retaliation for his crimes. And we can all imagine the reaction of the western political-media class if that had happened.

Speaking of Netanyahu, a new report from the Israeli outlet Ynet says that after the October 7 attacks the prime minister angrily ordered the IDF to massively expand its bombing campaign without intelligence on who they were hitting, demanding that they just bomb as many buildings as possible entirely for the sake of bombing them.

According to the report, on October 9, 2023 the IDF told Netanyahu that they were bombing 1,500 targets per day because that's what they had the intel to justify, and Netanyahu angrily demanded to know why they weren't launching 5,000 airstrikes instead, telling them "I'm not interested in targets. Take down houses, bomb with everything you have."

So that's what Israel has been up to lately. It's just getting uglier and uglier, and people who purport to stand for equality and justice are having a harder and harder time squaring their ideological positions with their steadfast support for the genocidal apartheid state.

Liberal Zionists like Bernie Sanders have tried to reconcile their support for Israel by pinning the blame entirely on Netanyahu. A recent tweet by Sanders reads, "Netanyahu has not allowed any aid into Gaza in 22 days. He broke the ceasefire, resuming a bombing campaign that has killed more than 50,000 people. Now he is threatening a long-term occupation of Gaza. NO MORE MILITARY AID TO NETANYAHU'S WAR MACHINE."

One of the biggest scams being peddled by Democrats today is this frantic campaign to spin Netanyahu as meaningfully separate and distinct from everything Israel is — instead of the perfect embodiment of it — to protect Israel's image while it commits genocide and ethnic cleansing.

They're working overtime to hang this whole mess on the prime minister, so that when it's all over and the final solution to the Palestinian question has been carried out, he can take the sins of the Zionist state and the entire US-centralized empire with him when he leaves office without anything ever needing to change about status quo US foreign policy. They're repeating the George W Bush playbook.

Netanyahu didn't create the genocidal racism in Israel, the genocidal racism in Israel created Netanyahu. He rode already-existing sentiments within Israel to power, and has relied on them to stay in power ever since. You could not ask for a better representative of everything Israel is than Benjamin Netanyahu — nor indeed a better representative of everything the US empire stands for.

Liberal Zionists are having a hard time reconciling their positions of antiracism and social justice with their support for Israel because at the end of the day western liberalism is just as fraudulent and deceitful as Zionism is. We all watched them passively allow the Democratic president to turn Gaza into a pile of steaming blood-soaked wreckage and then demand everyone vote for his vice president. Democrats hold their worldview in place by psychologically compartmentalizing away from the atrocities their government commits in the here and now, while singing fondly about innocuous whitewashed historical revisionist versions of their civil rights heroes who died decades ago.

Democrats are an inseparable part of the US empire and its abuses, just as the US empire is an inseparable part of Israel and its abuses. It's all one big mess of depravity, with liberals tasked with the increasingly difficult assignment of placing a warm progressive face on one of the darkest chapters in human history.

Featured image via Adobe Stock.

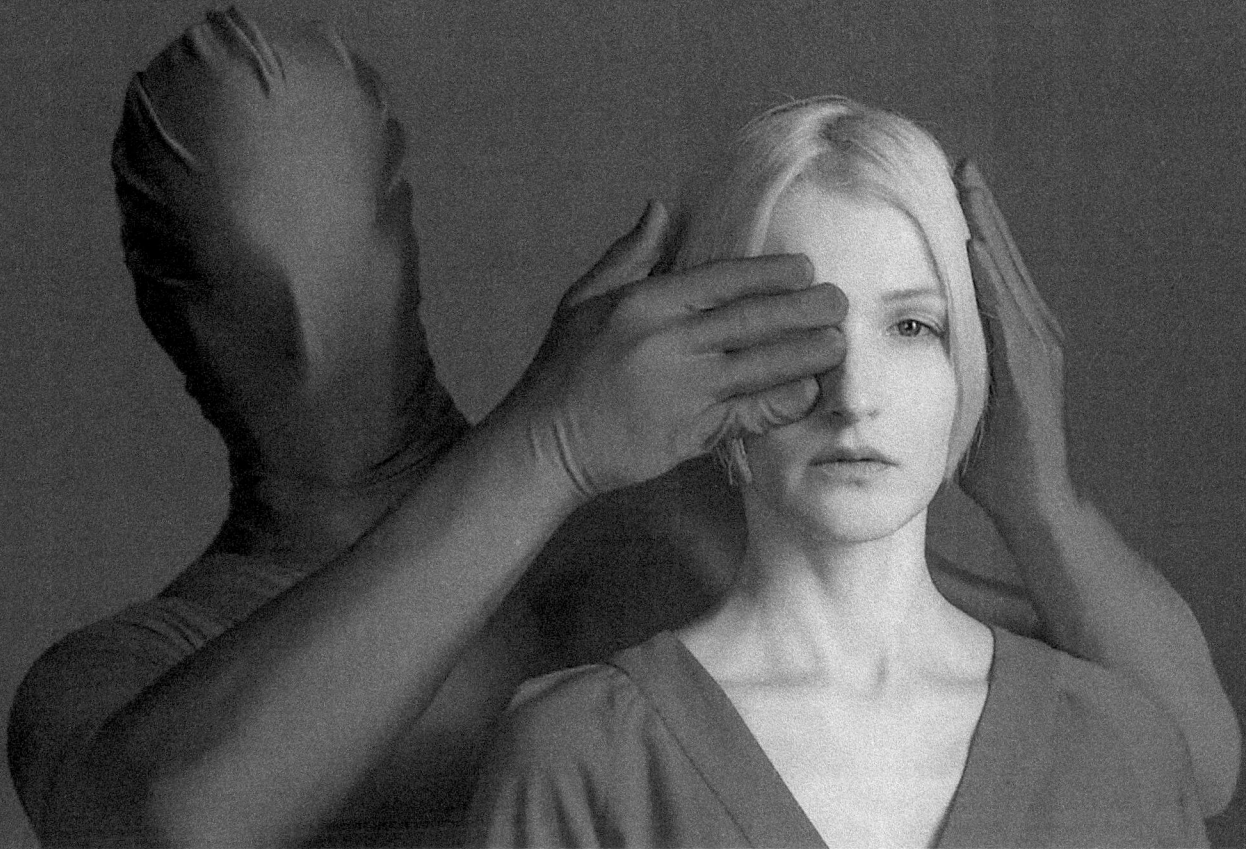

Censorship Violates The Rights Of The Speaker And Of The Hearer

The Trump administration is targeting another Columbia University student for deportation due to speech crimes against the state of Israel. This time they're going after a 21 year-old woman who was born in South Korea but has been in the US since age seven and is a legal permanent US resident.

The New York Times reports:

> "The student, Yunseo Chung, is a legal permanent resident and junior who has participated in pro-Palestinian demonstrations at the school. The Trump administration is arguing that her presence in the United States hinders the administration's foreign policy agenda of halting the spread of antisemitism."

This "foreign policy" narrative is the same as the one being used by the Trump administration's efforts to deport Mahmoud Khalil for his pro-Palestinian activism at Columbia; Trump himself posted on social media that Khalil and his activism are "counter to our national and foreign policy interests." The legal argument here is that because these activists are obstructing the foreign policy goals of the US government, it's okay to remove them because they are not citizens.

What people are missing about Trump's new policy of deporting pro-Palestine protesters on the grounds that their activism is contrary to US "foreign policy interests" is that it's not just an attack on the activists' political speech, it's also an attack on US citizens' right to hear criticism of their government's foreign policy.

As Frederick Douglass said, "To suppress free speech is a double wrong. It violates the rights of the hearer as well as those of the speaker." Even if you believe people who aren't US citizens should have no free speech rights and that it's fine for the US government to deport them for criticizing its actions, you can't use that same logic to argue that the US government should also have the right to prevent US citizens from hearing those criticisms.

But that's exactly what the Trump administration is doing. By making it clear that it is deporting pro-Palestinian activists not for any crime but for obstructing their "foreign policy goals", they are admitting that they are taking action to stop Americans from hearing criticisms and objections to their own government's actions in the middle east. It's tantamount to blocking Americans from reading certain political books or viewing certain political websites because the criticisms of US foreign policy contained therein might contaminate them with wrongthink.

Governments around the world inflict this sort of censorship all the time, but the United States is supposed to have constitutional restrictions on Washington's ability to violate people's freedom to hear dissenting political speech. And until very recently, patriotic conservative Americans tended to pride themselves in those freedoms their country provides. But apparently they're willing to light the whole thing on fire as long as it advances the interests of the state of Israel.

Americans who are not fully brainwashed into the cult of Trumpism should be asking themselves if this is the kind of country they want to live in, though. Do you really want your government deciding what kind of political speech you are allowed to hear, and protecting your fragile little mind from wrongthink? Or do you want to decide such matters for yourself?

Featured image via Adobe Stock.

Pete Hegseth   Today

VP:

I understand your concerns — and fully support you raising w/ POTUS. Important considerations, most of which are tough to know how they play out (economy, Ukraine peace, Gaza, etc). I think messaging is going to be tough no matter what — nobody knows who the Houthis are — which is why we would need to stay focused on: 1) Biden failed & 2) Iran funded.

Thoughts On The Trump Team's Signal Chat About Bombing Yemen

The Atlantic has published the full contents of a Signal chat from earlier this month featuring top Trump administration officials discussing the bombing campaign the president was about to begin in Yemen.

There's a whole scandal in mainstream US politics right now about the Trump team's carelessness in letting the conversation become public. The story goes that Trump's national security advisor Mike Waltz accidentally included in the chat Atlantic editor-in-chief Jeffrey Goldberg, who then swiftly exited instead of staying and doing some actual journalism by observing what these warmongering swamp monsters were up to. Goldberg did this because he is not actually a journalist, he is one of the most virulent war propagandists working in US media today, having famously worked to manufacture consent for the invasion of Iraq by publishing false narratives linking Saddam Hussein to Al Qaeda. He is also a former IDF prison guard.

What's getting a lot less discussion in mainstream political discourse is the depraved nature of the bombing itself, and the Trump team's exuberance about murdering civilians seen in the brief exchange of messages. Waltz describes to the group how US forces waited until a target entered an apartment building and then flattened it with an airstrike, eliciting digital applause from the rest of the administration.

"The first target — their top missile guy — we had positive ID of him walking into his girlfriend's building, and it's now collapsed," Waltz said.

"Excellent," Vice President JD Vance responded.

"Great job all," said Secretary of Defense Pete Hegseth.

"Kudos to all — most particularly those in theater and CENTCOM! Really Great. God bless," said White House Chief of Staff Susie Wiles.

"Great work and effects!" replied intelligence chief Tulsi Gabbard.

Waltz and Trump's middle east envoy Steve Witkoff are seen posting numerous celebratory emojis.

Imagine how fucked up you have to be inside to react this way to the bombing of an apartment building full of civilians. How far gone you have to be as a human being. These are the kinds of freaks who rule our world.

Another thing that strikes me about the Signal chat is how Trump's supporters are so much more confident that Yemen needs to be bombed than Trump's own cabinet was. Any time I criticize Trump's ongoing war on Yemen I get his cultists in my replies going "Well obviously the Houthis need to be bombed to protect global shipping routes, what choice did Trump have?" But if you scroll through the chat you'll find mixed opinions about it, admissions that there's no urgent need to launch any strikes right away, and nonsense about how the bombings can be used "to send a message."

Trumpers have their tongues so far up Trump's asshole that they're more supportive of Trump's warmongering than Trump's own appointed officials.

In reality this entire conflict could have been avoided by simply using the leverage the US has over Israel to make it honor its ceasefire agreement with Hamas. The only reason Yemeni forces began attacking ships in the first place was to blockade Israel because of its genocidal atrocities in Gaza; as soon as a ceasefire was in place those attacks stopped, and the Houthis only announced that their blockade would resume again when Israel announced a genocidal starvation siege on the entire Gaza Strip. The Trump administration told Israel to let the US handle the Houthis for them, and that's exactly what happened.

But the main thing that stands out for me right now is a section of the conversation where Pete Hegseth talks about what the administration's "messaging" should be about the airstrikes.

Hegseth wrote the following in the lead-up to the strikes:

> "I think messaging is going to be a problem no matter what — nobody knows who the Houthis are — which is why we would need to stay focused on: 1) Biden failed & 2) Iran funded."

It's always fascinated me how much empire managers focus on messaging. Their focus is never on whether or not they should do evil things, it's on what narrative they're going to sell to the public about the evil things they're going to do.

Here we see Hegseth talking about the challenges in the administration's "messaging" regarding its upcoming bombing campaign on Yemen, and the need to establish a public narrative about how (1) Biden is to blame for it and (2) the Houthis are "Iran funded".

At no time does anyone ever raise the issue of whether or not it's ethical to rain military explosives on an already war-ravaged and deeply impoverished nation in order to protect Israel's right to commit genocide. Hegseth's interest is solely in what stories will be told to the public to justify those actions.

These are the kinds of people who rule our world. This is how they think.

The powerful understand that narrative control is everything. Power is the ability to control what happens, but ultimate power is the ability to control what people *think* about what happens. Human consciousness is dominated by mental narratives, so if you can control what narratives the humans believe about their reality, you can control the humans.

The need to control the narrative is why the US empire has invested so heavily in soft power, and why it has the most sophisticated propaganda machine ever constructed. It's why Palestinian journalists are being killed in Gaza while western journalists aren't being allowed in. It's why pro-Palestine activists are being silenced and deported. It's why the internet is being censored with increasing aggression. It's why Julian Assange spent years in prison.

The empire invests extensively in narrative control, as do manipulative people in general. If you've ever had the misfortune of knowing a malignant narcissist or sociopath, you'll know they tend to pour immense amounts of energy into manipulating the social narrative about themselves and the people in their circle. Manipulators understand the power of narrative control, while ordinary people do not.

And that's why the world looks the way it looks: powerful manipulators understand this dynamic, while the rest of humanity typically doesn't. Normal people tend to assume they're looking at a more or less accurate picture of what's happening and how the world works from the information that's laid out in front of them, not understanding that the information they consume is being constantly distorted, funneled and manipulated by the powerful to the benefit of our rulers.

That's how consent is manufactured. That's how wars are justified. That's how revolution is suppressed. That's how the political status quo is maintained. That's how the public is duped year after year into signing on to more of the same while being robbed, cheated, exploited, impoverished, censored, oppressed, brainwashed, and driven to environmental disaster.

The real currency of our world is not gold, nor bureaucratic fiat, nor even war machinery. The real currency of our world is narrative and the ability to control it. We will keep being manipulated into disaster and dystopia until enough of us wake up to this reality.

•

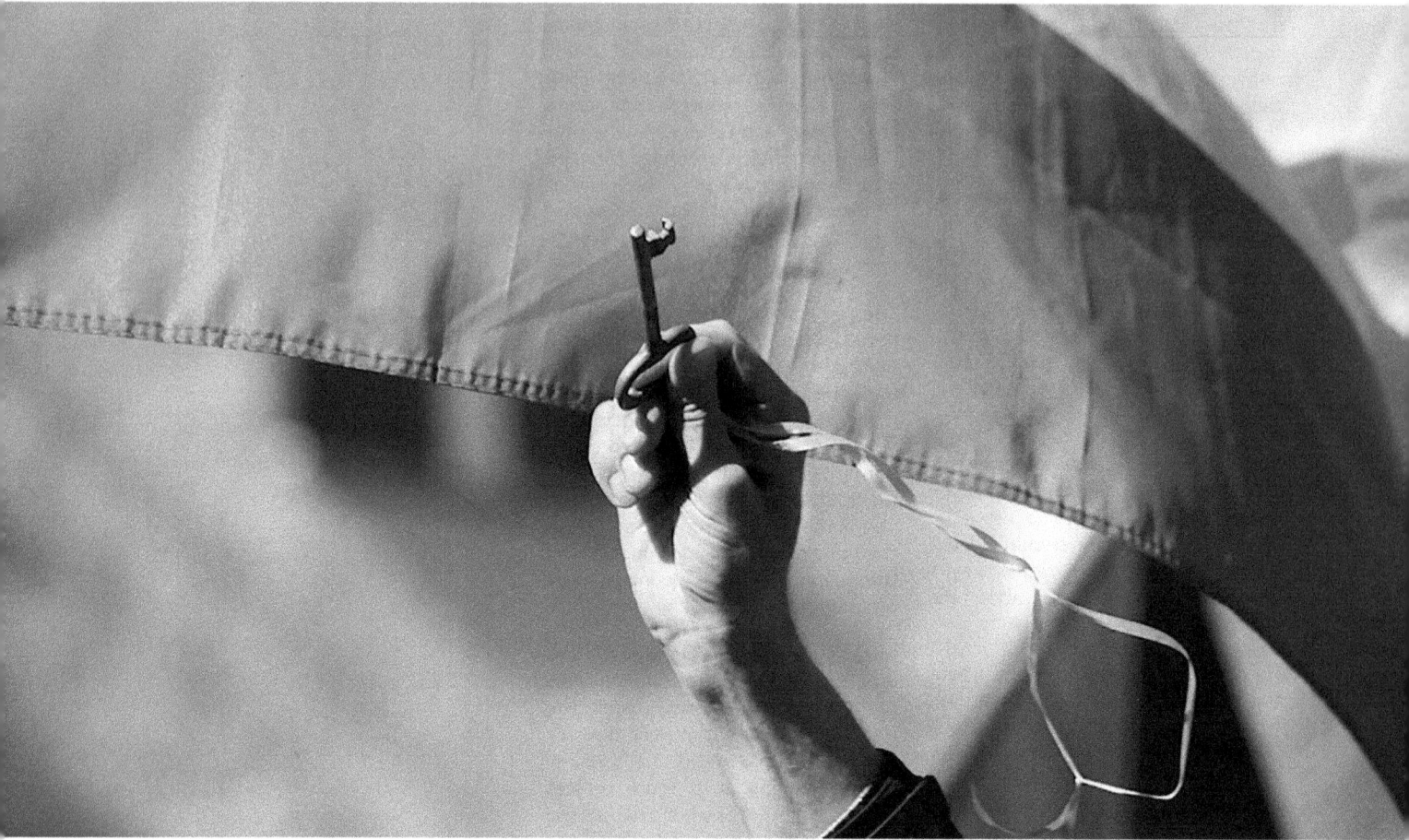

I Envy The Palestinians

I envy the Palestinians. Not for what they're going through, obviously, but for what they have. Their supremely authentic culture, with its deep roots and ancient connection to the land.

One of the very, very few good things that the Gaza holocaust has brought into this world is a deluge of footage of Palestinians living their lives, interacting with each other and relating to their loved ones as they find ways to get by in this nightmare. Westerners like me have been quietly watching these video clips on our little screens in our homes, and watching the various films, documentaries and shows that have been made about Palestinian life over the years, and taking it all in.

And it's just so very moving. Palestinians are such amazingly beautiful people. How tender they are with each other. How real and organic their spirituality is. How deeply they love their culture in all its unique expressions. How profoundly intimate their connections with each other are, both between individuals and with their community as a whole.

I'm a white Australian. We just don't experience such things. The indigenous inhabitants of this land were massacred, robbed and displaced just as the Palestinians are today, and my ancestors were brought to this continent from Ireland and Scotland by circumstances beyond their control. Now for the most part it's just this shallow, vapid civilization whose primary cultural identity consists of not getting too worked up about things. We live with this perpetual vague state of alienation and dysphoria buzzing in the background of our consciousness, because we have no roots here.

My husband Tim is an American of Irish descent and has had much the same experience. That's just what it's like for white people in the colonized world. We have no connectedness. No historical depth. No real culture. No real grounding. That's why we're always reaching around for something other than what we have, whether it's more money and more possessions or a return to the religion of our grandparents or New Age spirituality or substance abuse. Our experience here just doesn't feel quite right. We don't feel like we belong.

Then we look at the Palestinians and how starkly their society contrasts with our own, and we can't help but feel a sense of deep longing. They live so naturally and so warmly. It just looks right.

And I am quite certain Israelis feel the same way when they look at Palestinians. Here they are with this ridiculously fake culture of AI and electronic dance music, speaking a strange new version of a dead language that Zionists reanimated a few generations ago so they could LARP as middle easterners and pretend the "Israel" of today has anything whatsoever in common with the historic Israel of Biblical times. And then they look over at the people who were living there before them with their deep roots and vibrant authenticity, and they feel envy. And their envy turns to spite. And their spite turns to hate. And their hate turns to genocide.

There are other reasons for the hatred Israelis feel toward Palestinians, to be sure — the entire apartheid state depends on their being aggressively indoctrinated into viewing the lower-tiered inhabitants of the land as less than human. But jealousy surely plays a part.

And I hope they don't succeed in wiping out the Palestinians. I hope they don't succeed in driving them off their land. It would be such a loss to the whole world for a thing of such beauty to be snapped from its roots and cast into the dustbin of history. Apart from all the other reasons to feel heartbroken about the abuses we are witnessing in Gaza and the West Bank, there's the fact that our world is losing one of the most breathtakingly beautiful things it has ever birthed into existence.

If these freaks succeed in stomping out Palestine, I think it will genuinely feel like losing a loved one. I think many people around the world will feel the same way.

I desperately hope this doesn't happen. If I were a different sort of person with a different sort of spirituality, I would say I pray this doesn't happen. In a world that's increasingly fake and fraudulent, we can't afford to lose Palestine.

Featured image via Montecruz Foto (CC BY-SA 2.0)

Trump Supporters Can No Longer Say Trump Never Started A War

I'd like to point out that the tired MAGA talking point about how Trump "never started any new wars" has officially been invalidated because of Yemen.

The focus on "new wars" was always a dopey arbitrary distinction meant to shelter Trump from criticism of his extensive warmongering throughout his first term, but his restarting the US bombing campaign in Yemen in order to protect Israel's right to commit genocide means even this feeble excuse has gone up in smoke.

The US launched dozens of airstrikes in Yemen on Friday morning in its new offensive against Ansar Allah, who are essentially Yemen's ruling government since the territory they control contains some 80 percent of the nation's population. The US has bombed Yemen every day since restarting the war earlier this month, and Trump told the press on Wednesday that he intends to keep the attacks going "for a long time".

And when I say war, I mean war. When you are bombing a country every single day and announcing that you intend to keep bombing it for a long time, that's the thing that war is. You might not call it that, but that is in fact what you are doing. You are waging war on that country.

And make no mistake: this is a new war that Trump started. Yemen was at war between 2015 and 2022 against a US-backed coalition spearheaded by Saudi Arabia, but that conflict has been over for three years. Biden had been launching airstrikes against Houthi forces in 2024 in response to their Red Sea shipping blockade which was aimed at forcing Israel to halt its genocide in Gaza, but Ansar Allah suspended that blockade when a ceasefire was reached between Israel and Hamas, and the Red Sea had been peaceful.

That all ended when Trump began sabotaging the ceasefire and failed to use the White House's immense leverage to force Israel to abide by its agreement with Hamas. Israel announced a genocidal starvation siege on Gaza in full coordination with the Trump administration, and Ansar Allah responded by saying it would resume the Red Sea blockade to pressure Israel to halt its genocidal atrocities. Trump then began bombing Yemen before the Houthis had even launched any kind of attack, all to make sure Israel could commit genocide without consequences. The Trump administration reportedly even asked Israel not to respond to Yemeni attacks against it, saying the US would take care of the whole thing.

So there you have it. Trump started a new war, in every way that matters. There was peace, and then Trump actively sabotaged it, committing instead to a long-term war so needlessly that his own cabinet was seen in a leaked group chat questioning the decision and trying to come up with reasons why it was even necessary.

Face it Trumpers: you've been had. You voted for a president who told you he was going to end the wars, and he started a new war and was backing an active genocide within a few weeks of taking office. You voted for a president who said he'd protect free speech, and he's stomping out free speech throughout the United States to silence criticism of Israel. You voted for a president who said he'd put America first, and he's putting Israel first.

Mark Twain said "It's easier to fool people than to convince them that they have been fooled," so maybe I am wasting my breath here. But you have been fooled, my red-hatted lovelies. You have been fooled very badly.

If you can't accept it just yet, don't worry. He'll show you more proof before long.

Featured image via Trump White House (Public Domain).

The Word "Bombing" Means Different Things Depending On Where It Happened

The word "bombing" is interesting, because it becomes a different word depending on what part of the world it's being used in reference to.

If I look at you with a shocked and serious expression and say "There's been a bombing," you'll immediately assume I mean there was an explosion in a city near you, or perhaps in some other western city like New York or London. If you see me reading the paper and casually stating "Wow there were dozens of bombings last night," you'll probably assume I mean military explosives being dropped on people in the middle east.

If I was in the UK in the nineties and said "There's been a bombing," everyone would immediately assume I meant an IRA attack on British soil and respond with grief. If I made the exact same noises with my mouth in the UK today, people would assume I'm probably talking about Gaza, Lebanon or Yemen, and they'd shrug.

It's two very different words. They're spelled and pronounced the same. They have basically the same meaning. But they're different words. At least in the parts of the world where English is the dominant language, they have a completely different weight, and they land completely differently. One is shocking and horrifying, while the other is normal and expected. One will be the leading story in your news media for days, while the other might not even get mentioned.

The words have two different meanings in our society because western society does not regard non-westerners as fully human. An explosion of deliberate human origin taking place in our own neighborhood is an unacceptable outrage that we'll speak about for the rest of our lives, but the exact same thing happening in a neighborhood in the middle east is just the natural order of things — even if it was perpetrated by our own leaders.

Someone exploding a building full of pale-skinned English speakers is an earth-shaking tragedy, while someone exploding a building full of darker-skinned Arabic speakers is just Tuesday.

They're viewed as two completely different things because the victims are viewed as two entirely different species. The victims of the bombing campaigns the western empire perpetrates and sponsors are seen as subhuman. They are seen as subhuman because we've been propagandized to see them that way, and we are propagandized to see them that way because if we saw them as fully human, nothing about our society would make sense.

If we saw the inhabitants of the global south as fully human, it would not make sense for us to be extracting their labor and resources at extortionate rates for our own benefit. It would not make sense for our leaders to be staging coups, interfering in elections, and launching all-out regime change invasions to ensure they have governments which serve our interests. It would not make sense for the US empire to be setting up military bases in and around their countries to ensure its planetary domination. It would not make sense for an entire industry of war profiteering to be built around manufacturing consent for needless military operations and military expansionism in impoverished nations. It would not make sense for western governments to be shipping their trash to developing nations whose populations are now drowning in garbage.

Our entire civilization is built around this division. The division between westerners whose lives matter and non-westerners whose lives do not. This split is the unacknowledged elephant in the room in most aspects of our day to day lives. It directly touches the products we use and discard, the energy we consume, the status quo political systems we talk about and vote on, the very device you're reading these words on. It's all made possible by the fact that our lives are built on the blood, sweat and tears of the majority of this planet's population whose lives are not regarded as fully human.

We like to think of ourselves as having transcended the evils of slavery and genocidal colonialism which ravaged so much of humanity in previous centuries, but we haven't. Not really. We've made it more sanitized. More photogenic. Now you can read about slavery and shake your head about how terrible it was while wearing and holding objects that were manufactured by the outsourced slavery of the 21st century. You can vote for a politician with brown skin or see someone of Asian ancestry play a character on a TV show and think nice thoughts about how far we've come as a society, even as your government drops military explosives on people on the other side of the world because they're not seen as real human beings.

Our species won't find health and harmony on this planet until we truly start seeing everyone as equal, and acting accordingly. This tyrannical, exploitative way of living is only driving us toward annihilation and dystopia, and poisoning the planet we all depend on for survival.

Featured image via Adobe Stock.

DNI Tulsi Gabbard ✔
@DNIGabbard

Follow

President Trump IS the President of Peace. He is ending bloodshed across the world and will deliver lasting peace in the Middle East.

US launches 65 airstrikes across northern Yemen in 24 hours

The US claims the operations targeted Houthi rebels but civilian areas were also hit, with one killed and four wounded.

The "President Of Peace" Just Bombed Yemen 65 Times In 24 Hours
•Notes From The Edge Of The Narrative Matrix•

The US launched 65 airstrikes in 24 hours in Yemen, and then Trump's intelligence chief Tulsi Gabbard tweeted, "President Trump IS the President of Peace. He is ending bloodshed across the world and will deliver lasting peace in the Middle East."

These freaks have no connection with reality.

•

I saw a video the other day of a father cradling the decapitated head of his son from an airstrike in Gaza, and I'm told I'm a terrorist supporter if I criticize the people who decapitated him.

•

The word "terrorist" is a meaningless tool of imperial narrative control.

Want to bomb some people? Designate them as terrorists.

Want to silence protesters and dissidents? Say they're supporting terrorists.

Want sweeping surveillance powers? Say you need them to fight terrorism.

•

The list of people the Trump administration is working to deport for speech crimes against Israel is getting longer and longer, and includes a doctoral student whose sole offense was writing an op-ed critical of the Gaza holocaust.

Republicans spent years whining that government is too big and free speech is dying and everyone's too weak and sensitive, only to turn around and applaud the government for stomping out free speech to protect their delicate little ears from hearing wrongthink about Israel.

•

Two recent headlines:

"Israel admits firing at ambulances in Gaza," from The Guardian,

and

"Israeli soldier tells CBS News he was ordered to use Palestinians as human shields in Gaza."

The western press are only allowed to report on Israeli crimes when the Israelis admit to it themselves.

Half of the evidence of Israeli atrocities in Gaza comes from Palestinians filming their own genocide. The other half comes from Israelis telling the press what they've been up to.

•

The Democrats committed genocide. Now the Republicans are committing genocide. There you have it. Neither party is acceptable. Case closed. End of debate.

•

Trump is as evil as Biden. Biden was as evil as Trump. If you can't see this by looking at the raw data of the behavior of their administrations, it's either because you're looking at incomplete data or because you're letting your political biases do your thinking for you.

Both presidents are guilty of extreme evils, and you can't separate the evils of one from the evils of the other. Biden spent the latter part of his term incinerating Gaza, and then Trump began working to clear it of Palestinians. Trump managed to secure the Gaza ceasefire that Biden spent 15 months avoiding, but then he immediately began sabotaging that very ceasefire as soon as he took office. Biden has been waging a dangerous proxy war in Ukraine that Trump helped provoke in his first term, and now that he's back in office Trump is tasked with winding that war down to focus on new wars.

The crimes of the Republican and Democratic parties are inseparably intertwined with each other. It's not that they're the same — there are some differences — it's that they work in conjunction to advance the same evil agendas. Saying the Democrats are better than Republicans or vice versa is like saying the top teeth of the shark are nicer than the bottom teeth; they might look and function a bit differently, but they're used toward the same deadly end.

•

There are no anti-war Trump supporters. If you're still supporting Trump after all his insane warmongering, you're not anti-war.

•

Trump supporters get so mad at me for listing facts about what a warmongering Israel cuck their president is. That big uncomfortable feeling you're experiencing is called cognitive dissonance, fellas. It's what being wrong feels like.

•

The single most bat shit insane conspiracy theory I've ever encountered on the internet is that all the death and destruction we're seeing in the live-streamed genocide in Gaza is actually an extremely high-budget film studio hoax known as "Pallywood". Flat earthers make more sense.

•

If Israel doesn't want westerners voicing their opinions about it then maybe it should stop making itself such a central character in the story of 21st century western imperial warmongering.

•

Democrats pretended to support justice and oppose racism, then Biden exposed them all as frauds in Gaza. Republicans pretended to support free speech and oppose war, then Trump exposed them as frauds with his Israel policy. US politics is just empty noise draped over an empire.

That's all it is. The pundits and politicians could all be speaking in baby talk gibberish and it wouldn't matter. Presidential candidates could have their debates speaking Esperanto and it wouldn't change anything. The only reason they bother using coherent English words at all is so people don't get suspicious and start noticing that the politics of the United States are just empty noises fed to the public to let them feel like they've got some control while the tank treads of the empire roll onward.

It's like this in all western "democracies". The public is split into two equal factions who are then pitted against each other on issues that are guaranteed not to inconvenience the powerful in any way, and then the state just does what's in the interests of the empire without regard for any of the noises being made in the political sphere. And the brainwashed masses just keep babbling on about their politics, completely unaffected by the fact that the things their government is doing run squarely counter to the values they purport to hold. There's no real connection between the two.

•

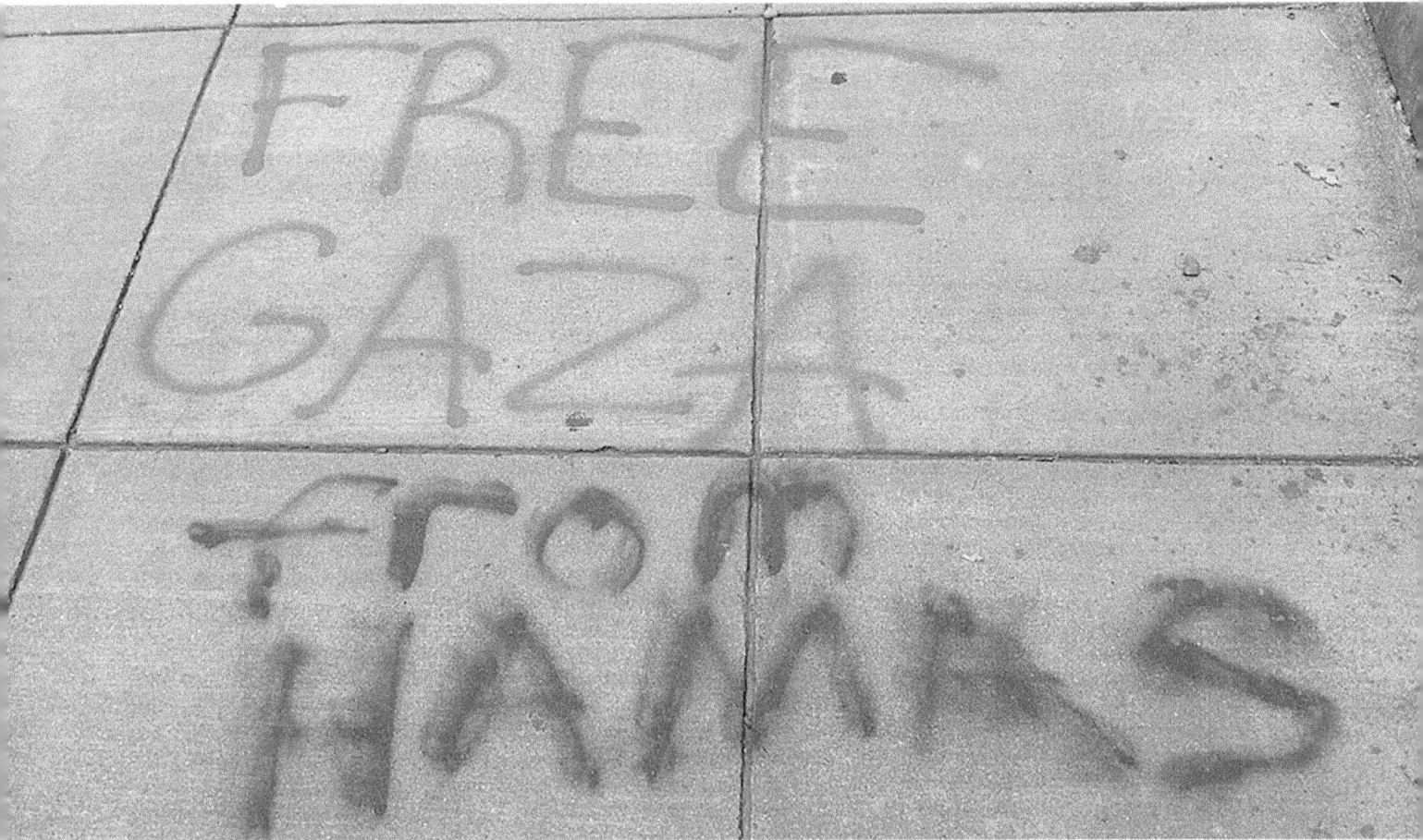

"Free Gaza From Hamas" Really Means "Free Gaza From All Palestinians"

Israeli Prime Minister Benjamin Netanyahu continues to insist that Israel will carry out Trump's ethnic cleansing plans for Gaza, saying the following on Sunday about "the final stage" of his agenda:

"Hamas will lay down its weapons. Its leaders will be allowed to leave. We will see to the general security in the Gaza Strip and will allow the realization of the Trump plan for voluntary migration. This is the plan. We are not hiding this and are ready to discuss it at any time."

Netanyahu's suggestion that Trump's plan for the migration of Palestinians out of Gaza would be "voluntary" is misleading in two separate ways.

Firstly, it is nonsensical to deliberately and systematically make a place uninhabitable and then claim that anyone who leaves that place would be leaving voluntarily. Israeli spinmeisters have been pushing this narrative since the early days of the onslaught, and it's transparently bogus; telling people they can leave or starve to death is exactly the same as forcing them out at gunpoint.

Secondly, Trump's plan for the ethnic cleansing of Gaza is not "voluntary" on its face. Trump has explicitly said "all" Palestinians are to be removed from the enclave and would not be allowed to return, which of course necessarily means that anyone who wants to stay will not be permitted to. Netanyahu says he wants to realize Trump's plan, and Trump's plan is forcible ethnic cleansing.

A Knesset member from Netanyahu's Likud party named Amit Halevi was just on Israeli radio saying that the plan is "to occupy the territory to cleanse it of the enemy," adding that Israel needs "to return to Gaza permanently and control this space, because it is part of our homeland."

I mean, how much more explicit do they need to be?

When Israel apologists respond to chants of "Free Gaza" with "Free Gaza from Hamas," what they really mean is "Free Gaza from all Palestinians." The agenda they are cheerleading has ultimately nothing to do with Hamas — it's about purging a Palestinian territory of Palestinians and replacing them with Israeli Jews. It's yet another Israeli land grab and yet another drive to eliminate Palestinians from their historic homeland.

If this was really about freeing Palestinians from Hamas, then why is Israel also seizing on this political moment to advance ethnic cleansing agendas in the West Bank, where Hamas does not govern? Defense Minister Israel Katz is on record saying of the occupied West Bank that "We must deal with the threat just as we deal with the terrorist infrastructure in Gaza," and the Gaza playbook is being increasingly utilized there. Tens of thousands have been displaced

as the Jenin refugee camp has been made uninhabitable under an aggressive Israeli bombing campaign, with hundreds of homes actively destroyed — not to combat Hamas, but to get rid of the Palestinians. Because that's all this has ever been about.

The western press have been obsessively covering the fact that some demonstrators in Gaza have been voicing discontent with Hamas, after those same press outlets just spent a year and a half ignoring millions of anti-genocide protesters around the world and running cover for Israel's mass atrocities in Gaza.

"Look!" we are told. "Those demonstrations prove that the people of Gaza want to be free from Hamas! This vindicates everything Israel and its allies have been doing!"

But, again, Israel's actions have nothing to do with Hamas. Hamas isn't the reason, it's the excuse. The excuse to advance an agenda that Israel has been trying to advance for as long as it has existed as a modern state.

This is what Israel's supporters and defenders are really advocating. Not the elimination of Hamas, and certainly not Palestinian freedom. They're advocating the end of the existence of Palestinians on Palestinian territory. No matter how much they try to sugarcoat it, that is their position. That's what Israel wants, so supporting Israel's actions in Gaza is necessarily supporting the ends toward which Israel is pushing.

Featured image by Ser Amantio di Nicolao via Wikimedia Commons (CC BY-SA 4.0)

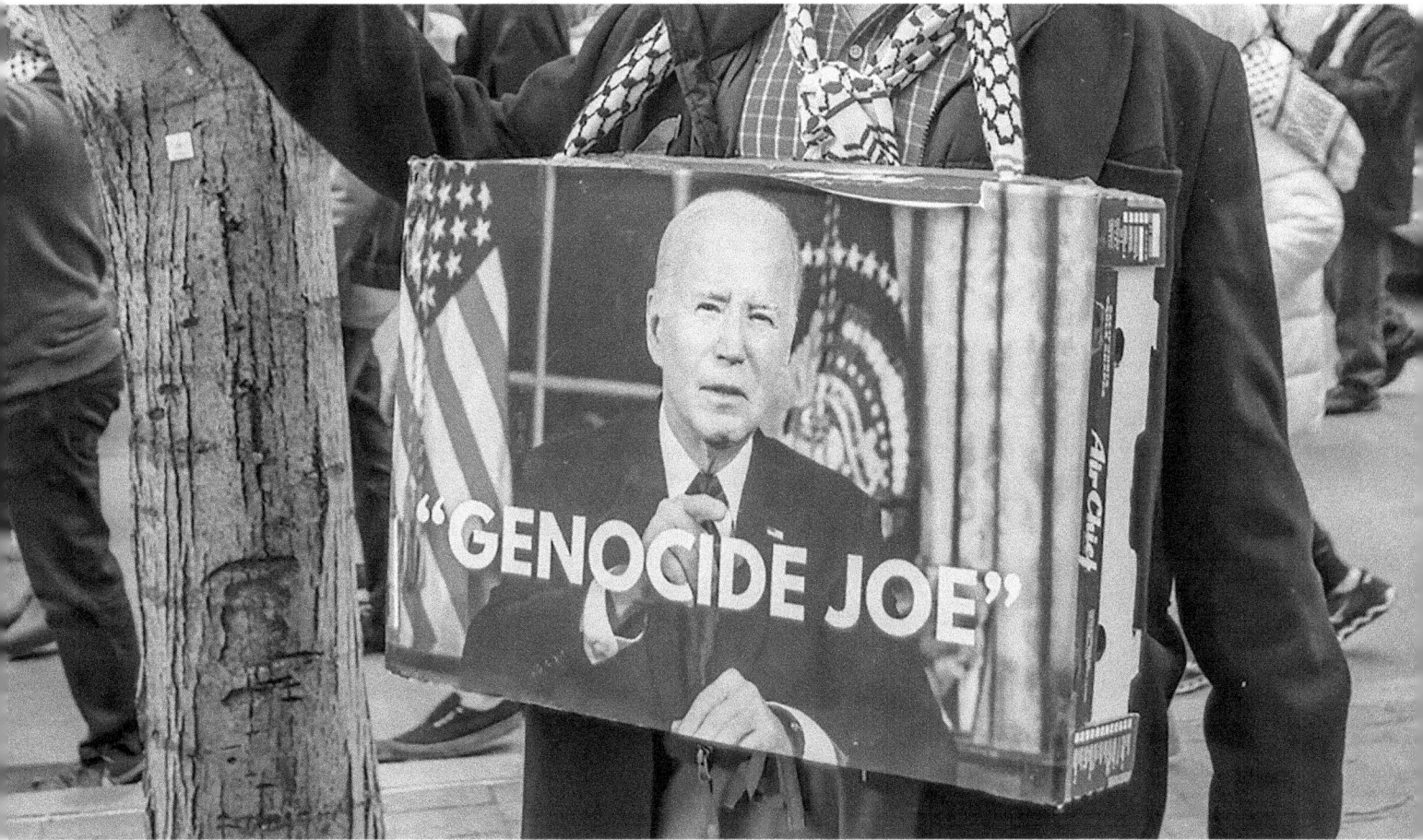

Liberals Believe In Nothing And Remember Even Less

The other day I shared a short post about a video that was going around showing a father in Gaza tearfully cradling the head of his son who was decapitated in an Israeli airstrike, and some guy responded with the comment "Good thing you helped get TRUMP ELECTED!!"

And I must admit I was actually, truly shocked. I mean, what exactly did this fellow think was happening under Biden that whole time?

I saw a post on Twitter where a leftist responded to a liberal who was acting like ICE just suddenly transformed into a modern gestapo under Trump, saying, "Liberals believe in nothing and remember even less."

And it's just so true. They don't believe in anything. They don't stand for anything. It's just a team sport for these people. Politics for the mainstream liberal is not about advancing values or building a better world, it's about their team winning solely for the sake of winning. And because they have no real values or causes beyond winning for its own sake, what their team does when it's in office doesn't matter to them.

A Democrat president can be as tyrannical and murderous as he wants and liberals will just brunch away in cheerful obliviousness, content with their knowledge that their team is holding the trophy.

You see this in the way our friend believes that I "helped get Trump elected" by criticizing the people who were perpetrating an active genocide. He just automatically took it as a given that it was my responsibility to stay silent on Gaza because the person in charge was a Democrat and his veep was running for president. The fact that it was a genocide which needed to be ferociously opposed never entered into the equation for him. All he cared about was winning.

All of the most shocking and gruesome things I have ever seen online were recorded in Gaza during the Biden administration. Nobody who'd paid the slightest bit of attention to Israel's US-backed atrocities in 2023 and 2024 would believe this was anything new that just started under Trump. But because Gaza is just seen as a political plaything by these freaks, they only care about it now that Trump is in office — and only insofar as it can be used to take points away from the Republicans.

And that's exactly why they lost. The Democrats calculated that the Harris campaign could simply ignore Gaza without putting any daylight between Kamala's policies and Genocide Joe's and still win the election, and they were wrong. Polls show that among people who voted for Biden in 2020 but not for Harris in 2024, Gaza was by far their biggest reason for not doing so. The Democrats believed in nothing and stood for nothing, and nothing is what they got.

Mainstream "centrism" is just as toxic, murderous and tyrannical as Trumpism. These people will watch entire populations being mowed down by the hundreds of thousands via the policies of the people they voted for, and as long as it doesn't interrupt brunch they'll keep sipping their mimosas and laughing and tweeting and feeling smugly correct, and then go to bed and sleep like babies in an ocean of human blood.

Feature image by Becker1999 (CC BY 2.0)

Trump's State Department Would Support Literally Any Israeli Atrocity

It's clear that Trump's State Department spokeswoman has been instructed to respond to any and all questions about Israeli atrocities in Gaza by blaming everything on Hamas, without even pretending to care whether the allegations are true.

For some background, Israel has just been caught perpetrating an atrocity so monstrous and so abundantly well-evidenced that even the mainstream western press have felt obligated to report on it. Outlets like the Guardian and the BBC are covering the story of how 15 medical workers for the Red Cross, Civil Defense, and the UN were apparently handcuffed and executed one by one by Israeli forces in Rafah before being buried in a mass grave. According to Palestinian Civil Defense spokesman Mahmoud Basal, they were each shot more than 20 times.

(As an aside, the fact that Israeli forces have been known to bury the victims of their atrocities in order to hide the evidence is one of the many reasons why the official death toll from the Israeli onslaught in Gaza is definitely a massive undercount.)

Asked by the BBC's Tom Bateman about these reports during a Monday press briefing, State Department spokeswoman Tammy Bruce responded by babbling about how evil Hamas is and how they are to blame for everything bad that happens in Gaza.

Here's a transcript of the exchange:

Bateman: On Gaza, the UN's Humanitarian Affairs Office has said that 15 paramedics, Civil Defense, and a UN worker were killed — in their words, one by one — by the IDF. They have dug bodies up, they said, in a shallow grave that have been gathered up, and also vehicles in the sand. Have you got any assessment of what might have happened? And given the potential use of American weapons, is there any assessment of whether or not this complied with international law?

Bruce: Well, I can tell you that for too long Hamas has abused civilian infrastructure, cynically using it to shield themselves. Hamas's actions have caused humanitarians to be caught in the crossfire. The use of civilians or civilian objects to shield or impede military operations is

itself a violation of international humanitarian law, and of course we expect all parties on the ground to comply with international humanitarian law.

Bateman: But there's specifically a question on any — it's a question about accounting and accountability given there may have been the use of U.S. weapons, so it's a question about the State Department rather than Hamas. Is there any actions —

Bruce: Well, every single thing that is happening in Gaza is happening because of Hamas — every single dynamic. I'll say again — I've said it, I think, in every briefing — all of this could stop in a moment if Hamas returned all the hostages and the hostage bodies they are still holding and put down its weapons. There is one — one entity that could stop it for everyone in a moment, and that is Hamas. This is — all loss of life is regrettable — it's key, obviously — whoever it is, wherever they live. And this has been the nature of what fuels Secretary Rubio and President Trump in their willingness to expend this kind of capital early on in this term to make a difference and to change the situation. So I think that's — that is the one thing that remains clear in all of this.

At no time does Bruce attempt to deny that the atrocity happened or cast doubt on the veracity of the claims, only justifying Israel's actions by blaming Hamas. Again, this is a story about medical workers being handcuffed and then executed by gunfire.

Tammy Bruce does this constantly; she did it in response to two separate questions at a press conference last week. When asked about Israel's assassination of Palestinian journalists Hossam Shabat and Mohammad Mansour, Bruce responded by babbling about October 7 and saying "every single thing that's happening is a result of Hamas and its choices to drag that region down into a level of suffering that has been excruciating and has caused innumerable deaths." When asked about the fact that people in Gaza have been unable to access clean drinking water under the Israeli siege, Bruce said, "Hamas did not perform to make sure that the ceasefire could continue, that they did not do what they said they would do. So we know, of course, when it comes to the ground water, of course, this is — it's a crisis. It's exacerbated by the fact that you have a terrorist group that just doesn't care."

She did it again at a press conference the week before when asked by journalist Said Arikat if the State Department considers Israel's use of siege warfare on a civilian population a war crime, saying "For the horrible suffering of the Gazan people, we know where that sits: it sits with Hamas," adding that the people of Gaza "have been suffering because of the choices that Hamas has made throughout the years."

Arikat, by the way, has just tweeted that on Monday he was not called on to ask a question for the first time in nearly 25 years of attending State Department press briefings. He is one of the very few reporters at the State Department who regularly asks challenging questions about US foreign policy.

So it's plain as day that there's absolutely no crime Israel could possibly commit that Trump's State Department wouldn't defend. Netanyahu could live stream himself kicking a baby Palestinian off a cliff and telling the camera he did it because he wants to commit genocide, and the next day Tammy Bruce would respond to all questions about the incident by yelling the word "Hamas!" with her fingers in her ears.

Bruce has a much easier job than her predecessor Matthew Miller, who under Biden was obligated to facilitate the Democratic Party's role as the nice guy face of the US empire. When the press would ask Miller about Israeli atrocities, he'd have to put on a whole show about how the Biden administration is in conversation with Israel and waiting for more information about these very serious allegations, all while fighting to keep his notorious smirk off his face.

To be clear, these two positions are not meaningfully different from one another. Pretending to care about very serious atrocity allegations while continuing to sponsor those atrocities is exactly the same as not pretending to care about very serious atrocity allegations while continuing to sponsor those atrocities. One is a pile of dead children with a smiley face sticker on it, the other is a pile of dead children with a frowny face sticker on it. The children are just as dead either way.

And you really couldn't ask for a better illustration of the difference between Democrats and Republicans than this. The Democrats are just the polite, photogenic face of the bloodthirsty US empire, while the Republicans are the empire unmasked. The Democrats commit genocide and ethnic cleansing while denying they're committing genocide and ethnic cleansing, while Republicans commit genocide and ethnic cleansing without bothering to disguise what they're doing as something else. One's prettier, one's uglier. That's the only difference.

•

https://www.caitlinjohnst.one